How to Talk to CHILDREN ABOUT ART

How to Talk to Children About Art

Françoise Barbe-Gall

CHICAGO
REVIEW
PRESS

HOW TO TALK TO CHILDREN ABOUT ART
Françoise Barbe-Gall

Library of Congress Cataloging-in-Publication Data
Is available from the Library of Congress

Originally published in France as
Comment parler d'art aux enfants
by Société nouvelle Adam Biro 2002
First Published in the English language by
Frances Lincoln Ltd
4 Torriano Mews, Torriano Avenue
London NW5 2RZ

Translation by Phoebe Dunn
American editor: Allison Felus
Copyright © 2005 by Frances Lincoln Ltd.

First published in the United States of America in 2005
by Chicago Review Press, Incorporated
814 North Franklin Street
Chicago, Illinois 60610

Printed in Singapore

ISBN 1-55652-580-X

5 4 3 2 1

To Yoram

For Emmanuel, Éden, and Raphaël

CONTENTS

INTRODUCTION

The aim of this book is to help people who enjoy paintings but don't know how to look at them share that enjoyment and talk about it with their children. The idea is simply to provide a few pointers. It assumes no previous artistic or historical knowledge or teaching experience. It is not an art history textbook; it contains none of the usual historical sections or specialist language likely to put readers off.

The world of painting is still rather intimidating. It can even be tricky to put one's most basic questions into words. It's hard to admit that you don't understand a painting that has everyone else in ecstasies—even if you are perfectly clear about why you like any number of others. Sometimes even our most logical questions go unanswered, mainly because we don't dare ask them, convinced that we are the only ones who don't get it—but we are not. This book explains some of those basic questions, providing answers that don't pretend to be exhaustive but aim to be as clear and as detailed as possible.

This book turns the traditional approach to art on its head. Instead of being presented with a lot of theoretical information on the period, the context, the artist, the subject, and so on, the reader sees the picture itself first. That's the starting point. This approach makes excellent sense since, for children (as well as nonexpert adults), the painting is always the most important thing. The painting exists firmly in the here and now, so there is no point in becoming sidetracked by preambles and digressions that might destroy any seeds of interest. What do you see and why? And how do you put that into ordinary, everyday words?

When preparing a visit to a museum with children or answering questions from a child who has seen a painting in a church, a junk shop, or a book, use this book in whatever way makes sense for you. Everyone will find different ways to satisfy her curiosity and different ways to read it to suit herself. According to the time or your mood, you might think that it's far too short, or alternatively that a single paragraph would have been enough. Dip into it, take it with you, read it from back to front if you want. If it leaves you feeling that the whole thing isn't so complicated after all, it will have done its job.

A GOOD START

Developing an interest in paintings

As with reading, an interest in art—and particularly in paintings—is not instinctive in children. It doesn't take much to kindle it, but it is also easily extinguished. So, it's best to be careful in the way you approach the subject.

Get rid of old habits

Even with the best will in the world it's easy to get off to a bad start. Who hasn't heard, or even said themselves, "You can't possibly visit that town without going to the museum," or "You must see . . . —it's beautiful." Such comments may be perfectly reasonable for an adult, but they won't appear to be valid reasons to go to an art gallery as far as children are concerned, and they are very unlikely to awaken any interest, let alone excitement. With such an approach to the subject, you are likely to be doomed to failure.

Think back to your own experiences

After all, are you really so sure yourself why it's worth the trip? What memories do you have of your earliest visits to exhibitions? If they are bad, or even just a bit dusty, it is best to keep them to yourself. The memory of boredom can be as contagious as boredom itself. On the other hand, if your experience was pleasant, try to work out why. Don't rationalize; forget all the knowledge and theory you've accumulated since then and focus on that first impression. That's the place to start; that impression, above all, is what you want to pass on.

Simply express what you feel

Even without thinking back too far, you can surely recall a piece of art, a place, a detail in a picture or a sculpture that really touched you. It might be something quite simple like a fleeting feeling, an atmosphere, or a color; it might have come from an exhibition or simply a picture in a paper. It is that emotion, more than any knowledgeable discussion that you should share with your child, using your own everyday words.

Something that stays with you

It will always be your own personal interest that you will transmit to your child. Tell a child that you like this picture, or that you don't like that one, that this one makes you laugh or that one intrigues you and he is likely to want to know why—

he'll want to uncover the secret. Better still, if you don't know why you feel the way you do, just say so. Ask his opinion, and with a bit of luck he'll tell you what to say. Always remember that no matter what intrinsic value others attach to a painting, the subjective value you put on it is what counts for a child. What you say is very powerful; it's not about school-type teaching but about sharing a confidence and the trust that goes with that.

Hold yourself back

Above all don't go on too much about what you are going to show your child. You'll deny him the pleasure of discovering it for himself. Whatever age you are there is nothing more annoying than hearing people go on and on about something you don't know about or haven't seen, read, or visited yet. So you need to rein in your own enthusiasm; otherwise the child may feel he is entering your personal territory and that there is no room for him. If you have given him exhaustive explanations of your pleasure, your emotions, and your opinions, what is there left for him? Give him the space and the silence to find his own words. Of course, if you just stand silently in front of a painting you want a child to appreciate, you are unlikely to be convincing, but talking too much and too confidently about what you know can be even worse.

Let the child choose

If the child doesn't share your enthusiasm, let him take the lead. Once you've done so, you have to trust his priorities; your preferences will have been a starting point but that is all. Notice what catches his eye. Follow him from room to room until he stops in front of something that speaks to him, even if he walks straight past something that, for you (and no doubt for others), is a masterpiece. You can always come back to the masterpiece another time. Your goal is to facilitate, to set up an encounter; it isn't really within your power to determine when or where that encounter will take place. The child's choice may surprise or disconcert you and it may even run counter to your own tastes, but it is nevertheless absolutely the best place to start, whether it's a nineteenth-century landscape or a 1960s monochrome.

Start where the child wants to start

Leave the question of where to start to one side. At this point the idea is not to embark on a methodical apprenticeship covering chronology, the stories of civilization, or artistic styles. Right now your only aim is to give her pleasure, the simple but rare pleasure of seeing well. Learning that you are free to look at exactly what you want and for as long (or as short) a time as you want is one of the major conditions for such a pleasure.

Tips for successful visits

If you want your visit to a museum, an exhibition, or an art gallery to be both fun and worthwhile, it is best to bear in mind a few simple rules—rules so simple that they are often ignored.

Forget rainy-day visits

Many people tend to think that a rainy afternoon is a good time to visit a gallery. On holiday, for example, they assume that if the sun is shining the family would prefer to do almost anything other than being shut up indoors with paintings. This is not a good idea. It supposes that going somewhere like a gallery is a last resort when every other activity has been ruled out. A visit to a gallery should be a positive choice, a reason to celebrate—it should never be a last resort. In any case, it's much nicer to see paintings on a bright day than on a gray day. There aren't many things more dismal than lining up to leave wet raincoats and umbrellas at the coat-check room.

Choose somewhere that's not too far away

We've all heard the cries "are we there yet?" on journeys with children. If the gallery you want to go to requires a long journey, it's better not to go. By the time they get there, the children will already be bored and fed up, and their spirits won't improve when they realize that they have to walk, as walking is still really the only way to get around a gallery. Even once you have reached your chosen gallery there may still be the problem of getting in. Lines can sometimes seem to last forever. If there is a line, you can either be patient or come back another day. But once you are in, don't hurry to the exhibits: take the time for a little detour to the café first. Your visit might improve with a little refreshment before you start.

Don't stay too long at the gallery (don't try to see everything)

No matter what kind of gallery or museum you've chosen, a visit will be an effort for a child. Walking slowly, being quiet, and not touching anything are bothersome restrictions for children (for younger children, the large spaces in galleries seem to be much better suited to running around). Also, looking at paintings demands attention, and the shorter the time that attention is required the sharper it will be. It's a thousand times better to look carefully at one painting for five minutes than to trail around looking at everything for an hour. Always remember that after half an hour a child is likely to have had enough and the younger the child the shorter the visit should be.

Explain the rules

The basic rules are the same in every gallery or museum. You mustn't touch or get too close to the art, and taking photographs with a flash is forbidden. For children, such rules can seem arbitrary. You will have to explain that the rules are aimed at preserving the paintings for as long as possible. Some of the paintings are very old and have survived wars, fires, and floods, and are irreplaceable and very fragile. They have to be looked after very carefully. Avoiding touching them, even with clean hands, makes sure that they don't get scratched or collect invisible but harmful microbes. Camera flashes create a bright light, which, over time, could result in a painting being "burned." Some places simply ban cameras altogether so that the temptation doesn't arise.

Put yourself in your child's place (and at their height)

In galleries paintings are hung to be viewed by adults. If you get down to child height, you will realize children can't see exactly the same things as you. Remember this. It might help you understand why a child is interested in a certain detail that might seem secondary to you; maybe it's at his eye level.

Use the maps and read the notes

Most galleries provide maps for visitors. If you let them, children will enjoy finding their way around. Older children might be interested in how the paintings are laid out in the rooms. Have they been hung in chronological order or do they follow a theme? Is there a focus on a particular artist or country? Have paintings been brought together from different eras or are they by different artists? Children won't necessarily instinctively read the informative little cards alongside each of the works displayed. You could point them out to them, and help them to decipher the exact names of the paintings, the artist's name and dates, as well as key technical information such as "oil on wood" or "oil on canvas."

Don't hesitate to go back to the same works

As with a favorite story that they never tire of hearing or a video that they can watch over and over again, once children have seen a painting they like they often want to see it again. So don't think it's a waste of time if you end up doing the same circuit every time you go to the gallery. The phase won't last forever and ritual is important early on. The favorite painting will act as an introduction to others. With your help, the child will understand that it is possible to see the same painting over and over again and to discover something new about it each time.

Buy some postcards at the end of the visit

Consider leaving enough time at the end of your visit to buy some postcards, and bear in mind that choosing sometimes takes a while! Postcards make great souvenirs and have the advantage of being portable. They can be stuck on a bedroom wall or used as bookmarks, they can be lost and rediscovered. Your child can collect them or scatter them about. Picking them out at the gallery can be fun, and later on they provide an easy way to develop a familiarity with the work.

What to show them, depending on their age

There is no point in setting limits on what to show children. Any picture has the power to speak to a child. We tend to think that a child will be more sensitive to abstract art ("it looks like a child's painting"), and that it isn't worth looking at paintings of unfamiliar subjects. That's wrong. Try. You'll be surprised how perceptive children can be about paintings. Their daily life is a world of images, and, without realizing it, they will have learned all sorts of visual mechanisms that belong to the ancient tradition of painting. Bear this in mind, and try not to pass value judgments on the pictures they like, as opposed to the ones you think they ought to like.

The following suggestions aim to clarify a few points and help you choose where and what to visit. They are a reminder of the kinds of things that generally hold children's attention, but should in no way be interpreted as definitive. As long as a child is old enough to be interested in picture books, he has the capacity to look at paintings and enjoy them. The material is broken down into three age groups: [red] five to seven years old, [yellow] eight to ten years old, [blue] eleven to thirteen (and beyond). These are not rigid distinctions but guidelines to be used flexibly according to the level of maturity of each child. Each of the three age groups is marked by a color, and for easy reference this color coding is also used in the commentaries in the third part of the book, How to Look at a Picture.

5–7-YEAR-OLDS

What attracts them:

- Warm, bright colors. Statistics show that a small child's favorite color tends to be red.
- Strongly contrasting shapes and colors, without shades (as in Legos).
- The appearance of relief because it "looks real."
- Art that reproduces textures (fabric, hair, fur, etc.), engaging the sense of touch as well as sight.
- Pictures of people—a lady, a baby, etc.—and of familiar places—a house, countryside, a garden, a village, a beach, etc. (subjects often found in Impressionist paintings).
- Pictures of movement and familiar poses: someone running, sleeping, diving, falling, dancing, etc.
- Clear expressions of emotions—love, laughter, crying or surprise—in paintings of any period.
- Simple compositions with one central person and very few other elements.
- Minute details. These are often what they notice first.

Don't forget:

Links with everyday life

Children of this age like pictures in which they can recognize events, objects, and gestures that they encounter in everyday life. For example, a child might see in a painting the position her mother adopts when she leans forward to brush her teeth or the way her father looks when he's working in his study. Another might like the red blanket in the van Gogh (21) because it looks like one he has at home.

Links with their bodies

Very small children don't look just with their eyes. Their whole bodies join in. They very quickly mime what they see and can describe pictures with gestures, embodying the image. That is when they will find the words to describe the ideas or feelings they have. Very expressive pictures or sculptures are best to encourage this kind of approach.

The realm of the imagination

When they see a picture, small children will often invent their own story to go with it: "She must be crying because . . ." "Maybe he's just done . . ." When they see abstract paintings they often link the colors and shapes to actual objects; a yellow mark will become a sun or a moon, while a curvy shape will be a snake or a banana. That bit of green that doesn't mean anything in particular to you will become a blade of grass or a jumping frog. It's their way of owning what they see. As long as children are allowed plenty of scope to interpret as they wish, abstract art (painting, sculpture, or installation) arouses their curiosity. Even the most banal or unexpected materials (twigs, bits of plastic, trash, pebbles, etc.), which are often used in contemporary art, can be very evocative for children and provide a springboard for young imaginations.

Giving things names

No matter what they are looking at it's always possible to help children's interest along with simple questions: "Don't you think that . . . ?" "What does that make you think of?" "How does that make you feel?" "Have you ever seen anything like that?" "I think that . . ." You can help them grasp ideas such as light/dark (chiaroscuro), heavy/light, transparent/opaque, fat/thin, precise/vague that they can use later on when they're looking at other paintings. The best start is to train them to see well while allowing their imaginations free rein and showing them that each picture is unique.

Books are better than museums

Very young children find visits to museums and galleries tiring. They have short attention spans. On the other hand, they love looking at books, which can present possibilities for games that might not be appropriate at a museum. If you are looking at a book about Mondrian, for example, find a picture with red, yellow, and blue in it. As you turn the pages, the reds disappear and come back later, while the yellows disappear, too. Watching, waiting, searching, and finding again can be a game in itself, applicable not just to colors but also to shapes, poses, or figures; this kind of game works equally well with photos of sculptures. Looking at the book together is the important thing at the beginning; it can be as special as a bedtime story. If a child seems to prefer a particular work or type of work, it obviously makes sense to go and see it "for real," if you can. It will be a treat.

8 – 10-YEAR-OLDS

What they like:
- Paintings full of color and/or contrast: these are as pleasing to this age group as they are to younger children.
- Pictures with a story behind them—a story of either the subject or of the artist.
- Clearly drawn character types: good guys, bad guys, heroes, underdogs, etc. These types appear again and again in the films, cartoons, and video games they already know.
- Situations of conflict where good wins over evil.
- Heroes.
- Pictures that make you laugh or make fun of others.
- Scary pictures.
- Strange- or monstrous-looking people.
- Images depicting daily life in different eras.

Staying in front of a painting long enough to feel part of it. Landscapes can be particularly good at drawing youngsters in. They can imagine making their way through the valleys, getting lost in a storm, doing battle with strange monsters, and boarding sailing ships. They're a great way to capture their imagination.

Don't forget:

Use their visual reference points
Children's visual world, which won't necessarily be highly aesthetic, is peopled with characters from films, video games, and cartoons, which tend to be heroic. Take advantage of these characters to talk about the principles they illustrate. If you are talking about good and evil, for instance, you could use Star Wars or Spider-Man as examples. Such ideas are behind many aspects of painting or sculpture, particularly in mythological or biblical subjects.

Getting to know the museum

This is the best age to start visiting museums and galleries. There's something exciting about making a trip somewhere to see something special.

Information to be discovered for themselves

It's very affirming for children to be able to read for themselves the little notices next to each piece and to find out the name of the artist, the title of the work, dates, and the other information that might be listed there. With your help they'll soon learn to tell the difference between the inventory number and the artist's date of birth and many other helpful tricks. It's much more fun for them to find out the information themselves than to hear you read it out loud. It gives them a feeling of independence.

"How did they do that?"

This age group has much more curiosity about materials and technique than the younger age group. They particularly like paintings, sculptures, or installations in which they can see brushstrokes, scissor cuts, fingerprints, etc., since they should already be used to recognizing such things from their own elementary school art projects. This is the time to get them used to looking at a work independent of its subject and to get them interested in artists' techniques. If there are amateur painters copying masterpieces in the museum, watch how they work (without disturbing them). If you can, go and visit artists' workshops—engraving, pottery, or weaving. Watch restorers—of buildings or stained-glass windows—at work.

11–13-YEAR-OLDS

What interests them:

- The artist's personality and the main points of the artist's life.
- Why a picture was painted at a particular point in an artist's life.
- The way a picture is put together—for example, the illusion of depth created by the use of perspective.
- The technique used by the artist or sculptor to visually express a feeling or an idea. For example, what gives the impression of movement, even though the figures are immobile? What evokes the idea of authority or produces harmony in a portrait? How has reality been stylized in order to make it more intense?
- The time it takes to produce a work.
- Symbols, which, once deciphered, give access to a whole network of hidden meanings. (Why is there a dove in this painting? What does the lighted candle mean?)
- Comparing works by the same artist. Self-portraits are particularly good for this: especially Rembrandt, van Gogh, and Gauguin. Whatever the subject matter, it's also a way of learning to recognize the characteristics of various periods in an artist's career.
- Comparing works by different artists that deal with the same or similar subject matter (spotting the similarities and the differences).
- The relationship between a work and an artist and/or history. Even if it's just to draw parallels, you can start to make links with books or history lessons from school to add context.
- How much a work costs.

Don't forget:

They're starting to have less free time

This is partly because of their increasing workload at school. It's all the more reason to be focused about what you want to share with them, without giving them the impression either that they're wasting time or that they're having extra lessons.

They are losing some of their spontaneity

They already know all sorts of things and tend to leap to conclusions about what they see ("'It's stupid," "It's badly done," or "What's the point?"). If you tell them they are wrong you'll soon shut down any dialogue. It's better to be open: ask their opinion, share information, ask questions yourself, and compare. This is a gentle way to get them to see what they may have missed in the first place.

Some subjects embarrass them

They are at an age when nudity makes them feel uncomfortable, but you don't have to avoid or ignore it. The best thing is to focus on the meaning of the painting (the nudity of heroes, the symbolic link with truth, the changes in fashion as far as proportions are concerned, developments in anatomical research, how realistically the skin has been painted, etc.).

Images from advertising

Young people are very familiar with advertising images. They form a reference point for them. You can take advantage of the fact that advertising often uses the history of painting: make it clear that this is not a coincidence and help them to find images that have been used in this way. If you find a picture, or a detail of one, that has been used in an advertisement, you could go and see the original, or at least find a good reproduction. The Manpower logo (a perfectly proportioned man inside a circle) is borrowed from the work of Leonardo da Vinci; the graphics used on L'Oreal's Studio Line products are clearly based on Mondrian's paintings. You could also look at how the use of colors and the choice of poses in advertisements picks up elements of symbolism that have long been used in the world of painting.

The raison d'être of paintings

This is a key question. Discovering something that legitimizes a painting in their eyes will make children want to look at something that might not have appealed originally. In that sense, insights into the artist's personality begin to interest them. For example, looking at romantic studies of clouds might seem really dull to them. But if you show them how in the nineteenth century clouds were a means of showing the instability of emotions (they blot out reference points, they gather before a storm, etc.), you might capture their imagination.

The story of the artist

The history of art can be too general and too abstract for children; it's the history of the artists that they're interested in at the moment. You might have a chance to visit a museum or exhibition with examples of one artist's work or one even devoted entirely to that artist. The idea of the artist as "star" is not without appeal.

IT'S OK NOT TO KNOW

Sooner or later children will ask a really simple question that you have never considered before. Suddenly, you find you don't have a clue how to answer it. Most never bother to find out the answer. But who says you have to know everything? Let's start from scratch and ask some of those simple questions and lay to rest some misconceptions about all kinds of painters, the point of their paintings, and the subjects they chose.

The questions that follow, arranged by theme, have two main aims:

To move from the general to the specific: the discussion of museums and of paintings as objects (page 26) comes before questions linked to artists' work (page 31) and those about the subjects of paintings (pages 42–55) and the prices of paintings (page 56).

To deal with artistic subjects in the order in which they've developed since the Middle Ages: religious themes (page 42), then portraits (page 45), mythology and history (page 49), landscapes (page 52), and, finally, scenes from everyday life and paintings of objects (page 54).

An exception has been made for contemporary painting (page 36), which is dealt with at the end of this section; it seems like the natural place to cover the particular questions and problems associated with modern painting.

Numbers in brackets refer to the numbers of the paintings on pages 62–181.

Paintings and museums

Paintings haven't always been in galleries.

Every painting that's in a gallery has a long story behind it. None of them was originally painted with hanging in a gallery in mind. In the past paintings were used to decorate churches, palaces, or private residences and belonged to collectors. In those days you saw far fewer paintings all in one place, in an environment very different from today's galleries. If you consider that electric lighting has only been available since the end of the nineteenth century, you get an idea of what it must have been like to see pictures with golden backgrounds lit only by candlelight or how the intensity of the colors could strike someone viewing them in semi-darkness. These days, much contemporary artwork is conceived especially to be displayed in public places, which explains their monumental scale.

The "problem" with galleries of older art is that you see many religious paintings.

It's understandable that the majority of religious paintings can be off-putting for many visitors: what's the point in wasting time on pictures whose content does not correspond to your beliefs? Nevertheless, it is by using painting to spread its message that the medieval church allowed artists to develop a visual language: the placing of the elements in a painting, the choice and use of color and the symbolic use of light and shade were all developed originally in religious art. All these elements are still used in modern paintings. Avoiding religious paintings because of their subject matter means denying yourself access to a visual language that is widely used today.

What are the paintings made of?

The two key elements of any painting are the support (wood or canvas) and the paint itself. The oldest paintings were done on wooden supports (usually poplar or oak). From the fifteenth century (and, more generally, in the sixteenth century), the use of canvas made paintings much lighter, easier to store (they were less sensitive to changes in climate), and easier to transport (canvases could be rolled up). Paint itself is made up of pigments or colored powders and a binding agent or medium (paintings are described as in tempera or oil). Until the eighteenth century only naturally occurring pigments were used. From then on it became increasingly possible to produce synthetic pigments, and the number of tones available hugely increased. For many centuries the commonest binding agent was egg; paint using egg as a binder is known as tempera. From the fifteenth century oil began to be more widely used as a medium. Oil paint was more transparent than tempera and had a more liquid texture. At least until the twentieth century colors were almost always applied over a white or ochre base coat and then covered with a protective varnish. Contemporary painters often use acrylic paints.

What does the expression "mixed media" mean?

It means that the artist has used a mixture of materials (oil paint, acrylic paint, varnish, lacquer, etc.). Apart from the paint itself he might have used elements not traditionally included in a painting, such as fabric, paper, sand, wood, glass.

What other sorts of art can you see in a museum or gallery, apart from paintings?

Collections and temporary exhibits in museums and galleries might include works on paper, drawings, etchings, pastels, and photographs. Drawings are often preparatory sketches done at some stage during the planning of a painting. In some cases they are considered works in their own right. Because they are more fragile than paintings they are often displayed in darker rooms and shown for much shorter periods.

Are all wall paintings "frescoes"?

No. The term *fresco* is used to refer to a specific technique where paint is applied to plaster that is still damp (*fresco* in Italian means fresh). As the paint dries a chemical reaction ensures that the paint is captured within the base and its solidity is guaranteed. An ordinary mural is simply painted onto a dry wall and might even be done on a canvas that is then attached to the wall or the ceiling.

Why do museums have wall paintings and frescoes?

Even though they were originally painted onto walls in palaces, convents, or churches, some frescoes end up in museums or galleries. Before a fresco can be transported the layer of paint has to be removed from its support. That technique is still viable but these days it is more common to try to keep works in the places where they were originally painted or move them short distances if that is the most efficient means of conserving them.

Why are some paintings signed and some not?

It depends first of all on when and where they were painted. For a long time the subject matter and the home of the painting were more important than the artist. Medieval artists didn't sign their work because they were considered craftsmen (in the same category as bakers or pharmacists) who were simply applying their technical knowledge. In the Renaissance, during the fifteenth century, however, when the idea of the individual gained popularity and people began to consider painting from an intellectual standpoint, artists began to sign their work, but they didn't always do so. It was not until the nineteenth century that signing paintings became common practice. A signature is sometimes accompanied by the date of the completion of the painting and occasionally the place where it was painted. These days once again some paintings are not signed or have no visible signature. That's usually more for aesthetic reasons (a signature would spoil the painting) than from a wish to deny the identity of the artist.

Why are old paintings often so dark?

Some paintings were deliberately painted dark. For example, in the seventeenth century night scenes were very popular. But generally, darkness is caused by the aging of the varnish covering the paint. With time varnish can become yellow or even brown. These days, pictures can be made brighter by carefully lightening the varnish, removing one or more layers. Also, paintings that were exposed to candle smoke for a long time may be very sooty; these too can be cleaned. However, when the original colors have aged there is nothing that can be done to lighten a painting.

Do people repaint damaged paintings?

No, they aren't repainted, but they can be restored. That means they are cleaned, and, if a layer of paint is coming away from the support, it is reattached or the support itself is strengthened. If the painting suffers from a lacuna (a place where the painting has completely disappeared) that area can be painted using a color close to the neighboring colors and with small brushstrokes in the same direction. These brushstrokes should be visible to the naked eye. In that way even a very damaged painting can be made more pleasant to look at without cheating. Picture restoration follows three strict rules: it must be discernible (it must not be possible to confuse the restored portion with the original); it must be reversible (it must always be possible to remove the restoration work without causing further damage to the original); and it must use only stable materials (there must be no possibility of the materials causing further damage to the painting, either when they are applied or at some future date).

Why are some paintings protected by glass while others aren't?

Some paintings are more fragile than others. Glass reduces the risk of contamination by dust and any kind of physical contact. Paintings, particularly famous ones, can be targets for vandalism. Over the years many paintings have been attacked for various moral or aesthetic reasons: for example, Rembrandt's *Danae* in the Hermitage in St. Petersburg had acid thrown at it, and Velasquez's *Venus at her Mirror* in the National Gallery in London was slashed. So everything possible is done to protect paintings.

Do people steal paintings from museums or galleries?

It happens from time to time. Some are found relatively quickly and some are never seen again. The most famous art theft was that of the *Mona Lisa* from the Louvre in Paris, which took place on August 21, 1911. It was two years before the painting was returned. The thief, an Italian man, had wanted to return the painting to his native country, believing it to have been plundered during Napoleon's campaigns in Italy. Since then security has become a much more important consideration in all museums.

Who chooses the frames for old paintings?

Sometimes a painting is in the original frame, chosen either by the artist or by the person who commissioned the painting and never changed, but that is rare. Sometimes a subsequent owner might have chosen the frame, and the choice itself may be of historical interest. But generally the museum's curators deal with that sort of thing.

Why are some paintings in museums incomplete?

Many medieval pictures are from works with many elements: diptychs (with two panels), triptychs (with two side panels and a central panel), and polyptychs (with many panels). Sometimes certain elements have been damaged and may not have been preserved. Often the works have been dismantled over the centuries, as smaller sections were easier to sell to private collectors. Some canvases have been cut up for similar reasons. Now sometimes museums in different countries can own fragments of the same work. Adapting a painting to the taste of the time (chopping a rectangular painting into a more fashionable oval, for example) or to meet the practical requirements of the moment (adjusting the size of a canvas or a fresco to fit the space available, for instance) are other factors determining the changing of the format or shape of a painting.

Painters

What makes an artist "great"?

A great artist changes the way people see things—not just other artists but the general public too. He changes the way people paint. He goes down in the history of art as having presented a fresh, revolutionary way of looking at the world that touched a great number of people. His works are rooted in their time but over the long term prove to be beyond fashion. A great artist influences many others, becoming a model for other artists yet remaining inimitable. Leonardo da Vinci used light and shade (*chiaroscuro*) in a way no artist had done before him (6); Caravaggio transformed night scenes (10); Patenier developed the landscape (7); Degas captured the expressiveness of the body (20), and so on.

How did/do painters learn to paint?

In the Middle Ages or in the Renaissance apprenticeship would start very early. At about the age of six, children entered a famous artist's studio as pupils. First of all they had to learn all about preparing the colors (how to crush stones to obtain pigments, how to dilute them, etc.) before starting on drawing and finally moving on to painting. The whole process took several years, during which time the pupil served as an assistant to and finally as a collaborator with the artist. He became a master himself once he was considered able to earn and complete commissions of his own. He was then entitled to work under his own name and open his own studio, in which he in turn trained other future artists. This system explains why in the past painting was a family business passed on from father to son (or, more rarely, from father to daughter). In the seventeenth century academies were founded: academies were groups of artists for whom practical and theoretical lessons were organized. These were the predecessors of today's art colleges.

Does an artist have to be dead before he can be famous?

People often think that's the case when they visit galleries of old paintings. Such places tend to give the impression that "well-known painter" equals "dead painter," which fortunately isn't the case, as modern art museums and galleries clearly prove. Most artists whose work is in galleries today were admired and celebrated during their lifetime. But it's also true that hindsight puts an artist's work into perspective and allows us to judge more accurately the impact he had on the development of painting. So, if an artist has been famous for a long time, he or she is likely to stay that way.

Were the famous artists always famous?

Our appreciation of different artists can change over the centuries. Artists might fall out of favor because of changing tastes or the dispersion or destruction of their work. That was the case with Vermeer (15) and Georges de La Tour (11), both seventeenth-century painters, who were "rediscovered" by nineteenth- and twentieth-century art historians, after long periods of neglect. However, these periods were just hiccups in the history of their works, as we now know that both these artists were very popular when they were alive. On the other hand, van Gogh (21) remained completely unknown throughout his lifetime and only became famous after his death. The novelty of his work was difficult for his contemporaries to accept, but it was much more in tune with the tastes of the following century.

Why are there so many anonymous artists?

With the exception of ancient Greek and Roman artists (whose names and works we know from written records), writing down the details of a painter's life and work is a relatively recent phenomenon. In Italy, for example, it only goes back as far as the sixteenth century. Before that people only remembered the names of artists whose work was most frequently displayed. Identifying artists and correctly attributing paintings to them is made more difficult because works were rarely signed. Gradually some links have been established between certain artists and paintings through painstaking comparison between pictures of identical style, archival documents (such as inventories, receipts, and deeds), and even the odd signed painting. But most sources of documentary evidence have been lost or destroyed over time, and it's often impossible to attribute a painting unless new sources are discovered.

Why aren't there many female painters?

There are many female artists these days but in the past there were not because of the role women traditionally played in society. Social acceptance of women having a career at all, let alone becoming an artist, only really developed in the twentieth century. Nevertheless there are a number of significant female artists in history including Sophonisbe Anguissola (1530–1625), Lavinia Fontana (1552–1614), Artémisia Gentileschi (1597–1651), Élizabeth Vigée-Lebrun (1755–1842), and Mary Cassatt (1844–1926). Others have almost been forgotten or have not been identified, their work being associated with the studio where they were employed rather than with them individually. In the Middle Ages nuns and later the daughters of painters might have been artists, but women rarely painted in their own right. Beginning in the seventeenth century some female artists became famous within their own lifetimes. They tended to paint mainly portraits or still lifes, as they were forbidden to study with nude models. With a few notable exceptions, religious, mythological, and historical subjects remained beyond their reach. Female artists have been the subject of numerous studies by art historians over the last thirty years.

How do painters choose what to paint?

Until the end of the eighteenth century artists would work by commission. There was a written contract between the client and his chosen artist. So the subject matter was usually decided by the client, who specified his requirements. Today you can see fifteenth-century contracts that stipulate exactly what should appear in the painting: the number of people, the elements of decor, and the colors to be used, even in what proportions. The delivery date is also arranged, as well as any subsequent requirements made of the painter—a kind of after-sales service. The commission system has lasted and is still in use today, particularly for official paintings, religious works, or portraits of royalty and other heads of state, but it has gradually become less exclusive. In certain cases in the seventeenth century (10 and 14) and particularly during the Romantic period at the beginning of the nineteenth century, artists began to choose their own subjects. It was then up to the artist to find clients who both liked the paintings and were able to pay for them.

Is it true that in the past painters didn't paint only pictures?

In the Middle Ages, painters, as craftsmen, carried out any sort of work that required the application of paint to a surface. They were commissioned to produce paintings, of course, but also to decorate furniture, banners, and so on. From the Renaissance (fifteenth and sixteenth centuries) onward things began to change, but many artists still produced—apart from paintings—designs for procession decorations, festivals and events, designs for metalwork, and so on.

Were there often disagreements between artists and their clients?

Yes, regularly. There were often problems when deadlines were missed or the artist didn't stick to the client's demands. History is full of paintings that were never delivered (6) or were delayed for years because of disagreements over the size or the number of figures, the way they filled the space in the painting, or the failure of a painting to respect current ideas of decency. Sometimes the artist modified the painting as requested. If the client refused to pay for the painting it could then be sold to someone else. Sometimes the matter was decided by a committee or even taken before a tribunal.

What's the difference between a client and a patron?

A client is a customer for whom an artist works on either a one-time only or an ongoing basis. Their financial relationship is determined by the price of the work commissioned and delivered. That work can be anything, such as a piece of furniture, a building, an opera house, a garden, or, of course, a painting. The term patron assumes a closer link, suggesting long-term support for an artist's career or for an artistic movement. This sort of relationship flourished during the Renaissance but was rarely based purely on a love of art: the works themselves became symbols of a patron's generosity and open-mindedness, earning him a certain kind of cachet among his peers. In the same spirit, the world of business took to the idea of patronage in the twentieth century. Industrial companies and banks emerged as important patrons of the arts, mounting large exhibitions and financing restoration work as well as commissioning work and sponsoring competitions to encourage young talent.

How can a painter express himself when working to order?

These days it's commonly believed that artists create their work as a result of sudden inspiration and that they should allow their imaginations totally free rein accordingly. That's a romantic and somewhat simplistic idea that doesn't sit with the economic constraints and realities of the commission system that has prevailed for hundreds of years. An artist expresses himself whatever the subject matter and irrespective of whether it is close to his heart. An artist's creativity lies not in his ability to find a subject but in his way of treating that subject. The artist can conceive and establish a system of shapes capable of translating a vision and giving it meaning.

How did painters promote their work?

When a talented artist worked in a master's studio he quickly benefited from the master's network of clients, and his work—visible in churches, convents, or palaces—started to confirm his own reputation, which would then spread by word of mouth. Exhibitions as we now know them only really started in the seventeenth century in the wake of academies displaying their students' work. These exhibits were subject to the approval of committees but gradually artists started to loosen the hold of the establishment by organizing their own exhibitions. Near the end of the nineteenth century, exhibits and salons became increasingly popular, and private galleries started to open to display and sell paintings.

Did painters write down explanations of their work?
Did they really think about all that?

For many people the only thing that can really validate a painting is a written explanation from the artist himself. That idea assumes painting is somehow less eloquent than the written word. Painting is a language in itself. The artist's work is a visualized thought; he doesn't so much illustrate his thoughts as materialize them. Artists who have written about their work, as some abstract painters have, usually don't explain them fully, providing instead a sort of general clarification of their process and their thinking.

Painting in the twentieth century

What is an abstract painting?

A painting is called abstract when it doesn't depict visible reality. Instead of showing real or imaginary people, places, or things, it is likely to be a mixture of colors and shapes. An abstract painting doesn't "represent" anything: it simply "presents" itself. For some artists the conventional opposition between abstract and figurative art is not actually very strong: a picture resulting from some sort of reality (whether it be visual, emotional, or sensory) still contains that reality even if it doesn't illustrate it in a photographic way. Many paintings contain abstract elements alongside figurative ones, such as the 'puddles' of paint at the feet of Isabel Rawsthorne by Francis Bacon (29). On the other hand, for other painters the distinction between abstract and figurative is absolute. It can be claimed that the first abstract painting was a watercolor painted in 1910 by the Russian artist Vassily Kandinsky (1866–1944). That painting is now in the Musée Nationale d'Art Moderne in Paris. In more general terminology the term "abstract elements" is used to refer to any shapes or artistic forms not linked to reality, such as those used in Islamic art.

What is a monochrome?

A monochrome is an abstract painted with only one color. The Russian painter Casimir Malevitch (1878–1935) was the first to produce this type of painting in 1918, with a work called *White Square on a White Background*, now at the Museum of Modern Art in New York. Use of the monochrome technique is not so much an end in itself as a means of confronting the viewer, just as the artist has himself been confronted with the limits of figurative and representative art. Depending on the artist and the period, a monochrome work can signify very different ideas; from reminding you how opaque paint and painting can be to suggesting the emptiness of the cosmos. Painting a monochrome is an ambiguous endeavor balanced somewhere between stating the redundancy of painting and expressing the development of the art form (27).

Why are contemporary paintings often hung without a frame?

The abandoning of gilt frames in favor of white or colored strips by artists such as van Gogh, Seurat, and Pissarro at the close of the nineteenth century expressed a wish to democratize art and distinguish it from the bourgeois, elegant decor associated with such frames. Their painting was resolutely modern and dispensed with such old-style decoration. Then in the twentieth century some artists got rid of frames altogether, once again putting the emphasis on the self-sufficiency of the painting. Also, much twentieth-century art tends to focus more on the process behind the work than on the work itself: the lack of a frame underlines the idea that the painting is not so much unfinished as unfinishable. With no frame, the canvas appears no longer as an isolated object but as an open space.

Why is there sometimes no connection between the title and what you see in the painting?

Because we are used to the very precise names given to old paintings, either by the artists or in inventories, many titles in the twentieth century don't seem to make sense to us. They're not created to spite the viewer. A title need not just identify the content; it can recall the origin of the painting (something or someone who inspired it), initiate a discussion about how it is to be interpreted, suggest a state of mind, or give the painting a humorous or poetic slant. In many cases the name is much more than a definition: it is as much a part of the work as the image itself.

Why are there so many "untitled" paintings?

An untitled picture is considered to be strong enough to stand alone without any label. For some painters naming their work even risks diminishing its meaning. A title can often seem an unnecessary and artificial addition or an encumbrance. Free of a name, a painting can be free from all the expectations that would arise if it were qualified with words. The picture can simply exist, unlimited by and independent of language and any need to be verbalized. Calling a painting "Untitled" is nonetheless to give it a title of sorts. Sometimes the paintings are grouped in a series (*Untitled No. 1, Untitled No. 2,* etc.), which, as with musical compositions (Concerto No. 1, No. 2), invite the viewer to consider the artistic endeavor as a whole.

Why do so many painters do the same thing over and over again?

There is an idea that painters who always do the same thing are milking their fame for financial gain and perhaps concealing an inability to develop artistically. That's possible, but the theory ignores two key factors. First, painters are humans who have to eat. Even Renoir admitted that he would probably have starved to death if he hadn't painted all those pretty still lifes. Demand will always influence supply, even if it means encouraging an artist to repeat himself. Unless a painter happens to be independently wealthy, he will probably find it very difficult to resist producing what he knows he can sell. Second, the accusations of repetitiveness are most often unfounded. Many artists choose a limited repertoire because they want to explore every nuance of it. It's not so much a question of repetition as it is of the subtle and demanding art of variation. In a society governed by the cycles of fashion and the desire for perpetual change and novelty, the artist who mines one particular seam displays a remarkable level of independence. He has invented his own world and can discover depths in it undreamed of by others (27).

How can I tell if paintings I see really mean anything?

That's not the sort of question you would usually ask yourself in front of an Old Master. The clarity of the subject matter and the artist's technique are valuable enough in their own right: one Vermeer (15), for example, is enough to give a clear idea of the artist's worth. It's different for many contemporary works; modern paintings don't often appear as ends in themselves. A contemporary painting is more like a stage, a moment—like a word in the middle of a book or a stone in a wall. To appreciate the painting's full significance you have to see it in a context and evaluate it in the light of the artist's life, the trajectory of his career, and his relevance in art history. That's not always easy for the viewer, but temporary exhibitions and books can help. At the very least, you should remember that what you see now is usually no more than a short episode in a much longer process (24, 26, 27).

Why do some works look like a load of garbage?

Born from a consumer society, today's art often uses what society throws away. Rubbish is ever-present. After World War II, particularly after the explosion of the atomic bomb, the principles of how we represent the world were turned on their heads. With Hiroshima humans glimpsed their own extinction. Art began to evoke the idea not only of waste but also of debris, archaeological remains, and therefore, memory. Art can bear witness to a broken world by gathering together fragments with which to make its commentary on history. This technique, in its apparent simplicity, makes it clear that even the smallest detail warrants our attention, that the slightest tear or the thinnest layer of dust are worthy of being looked at as if for the last (or the first) time.

"It's badly done."

This kind of judgment is the result of a misunderstanding. These days we tend to expect paintings to have the same technical qualities as the Old Masters and certainly to use those qualities in the same way. It's a bit like looking at a woman in jeans and wishing that she had the silhouette of a marchioness in a crinoline. A painting that is apparently "badly done," that has an absence of modeling or proportion, that seems rushed or too tentative doesn't mean a lack of expertise on the part of the artist, but is explicable in terms of the kind of ideas the artist is trying to convey. Paintings don't work in the same way as stories or mimicry; instead they rely on parallels for their meaning. A painting's theme—chaos, solitude, innocence, etc.—is not depicted the same way it would be in a movie, conveyed directly through the expressive use of shapes and color (28).

"It's not finished."

The artist is the only one who can decide whether a painting is finished or not. No one else has the right to pass judgment on that topic. The fact that you don't understand why he stopped work at a certain point is one thing. His own motivation is quite another. The idea of completion in painting is not an absolute; rather, it's linked to history. If you think a contemporary painting doesn't look finished, you are probably judging it by criteria that are out of date. The appearance of being "unfinished" is often quite deliberate, signaling that a work will continue elsewhere, that it has only momentarily been interrupted. It suggests both the unsatisfactory nature of the work and the permanence of its impact (30).

"It's nonsense."

Just because you feel a picture offers no points of reference does not mean that they aren't there. Perhaps you simply have not yet been able to decipher them. Saying something is nonsense is to condemn it just because you don't understand it. To put it another way, we don't say that someone who speaks a language we don't understand is talking nonsense: we just need an interpreter. A picture is like a language and sometimes it's best to admit you haven't learned to translate everything yet (26).

"A child could do that."

Of course a child could produce a picture similar to some of those you see in museums. But most children would not have the emotional and/or intellectual maturity to conceive such a work. Children paint or draw spontaneously (just as they sing or dance), whereas an artist consciously develops a picture. One of the great challenges for an artist attempting to create a "childlike" painting is to use all the resources of his or her experience and visual and emotional maturity, without losing the qualities of childhood. What he or she is seeking to recapture is not the charm of lost innocence but the strength and absolute integrity of emotions as a child might experience them for the first time.

"Anyone could have done that."

No, they couldn't. The proof is that not everybody does. Nevertheless, when you're looking at an empty canvas with just a line or a few dots of color on it, this kind of reaction is understandable. Technically speaking anyone could create a monochrome without too much difficulty. But intellectually only a very few artists develop the vision to create a picture like that. It takes most artists many years to produce that kind of work and to expose him- or herself to the possibility of provoking an "anyone could do that" comment from the public. The ability to imitate such a work is not the same thing as understanding it; nor is it "creative," in the strictest sense. It's precisely the artist's act of creation that is worthy of respect—the fact that at a certain date and time someone so matured as to be able to produce such a work. There is a huge difference between painting and being a painter. Painting a picture does not automatically make someone an artist. Painting has to be a way of life, a way of interacting with the world. That requires a choice that is not suitable or possible for everyone.

The painter is making fun of the world.

Perhaps the artist is expressing him- or herself in a way that is unsettling to some viewers. People may feel they have been taken for a ride because they have a fixed idea of how a painting is supposed to make them feel. Nevertheless a viewer who feels cheated is forgetting one important thing: she probably isn't meant to be a target of mockery. Nothing can force her to look at or appreciate a painting. A painting does not impose itself on people. It simply is.

The Old Masters are "easier" to understand.

That's a fallacy. It's easier to identify the elements of the composition in older paintings, but that isn't enough. You still have to decipher the subject. An enigmatic theme—be it historic, literary, religious, or mythological—should leave a viewer longing to delve deeper. Simply recognizing the subject is not enough to understand the painting. If we recognize the *Mona Lisa* as a picture of a woman, have we really understood the painting? In the past you needed to know a certain number of codes to understand paintings. If you are fully to understand Uccello's painting of St. George and the Dragon (3), for example, you have to know that the knight represents good and the dragon represents evil. To understand *The Birth of Venus* (4), you need to know that Venus is the goddess of love and beauty and was born from the sea. These days painting calls on different reference points, based on modern history. It describes contemporary experience: the fear of destruction, hope, longing, death, revolt or desire, sensations or reflexes. These things are sometimes easier to understand immediately without any additional information.

What's called art these days is not art.

Saying that something is "not art" supposes that you have a clear idea of exactly what art is, that you believe the term can only apply to objects that are both technically and aesthetically perfect, and that perfection itself is an absolute, untouched by the vagaries of history. None of that is so. Since prehistory, art has played an important role in society. Although we don't know how they were used, we know that ancient humans transported pigments hundreds of miles from mineral deposits and that these colors were as important to them as their weapons. Painting was linked to their survival and had nothing to do with making things look pretty. Art can create a neutral ground between the internal and the external worlds, a place for an artist to express what she perceives, what she longs for, what she hopes for, what she fears, and what she rejects. Of course for a few hundred years painting also conveyed man-made ideals of beauty, but that alone does not define it. Painting (or art in general) doesn't limit itself to the search for beauty, even if it is a frequent theme and even if sometimes, sentimentally, we wish it could.

Why would anyone put *that* in a museum?

Museums usually acquire paintings because they are important either in the history of an artist's work or the history of an era. It's when personal history and the history of the times coincide that a painting really becomes significant. Modern art museums do not necessarily aim to be places for aesthetic delight only. They are also in some ways like laboratories, places where we put our environment under the microscope, sometimes distorting it.

Religious art

Why are there so many religious paintings?
For hundreds of years the art of painting in Europe really only existed as a function of the Christian religion, which played a dominant role in society. The Church commissioned and used paintings to spread its message. Books were extremely rare and many people did not know how to read. So, most people learned about the scriptures through paintings. Even then it was well understood that a picture touches emotions more directly than speech and impresses itself more on the memory.

What were paintings in churches for?
Church paintings showed people what they should believe in and gave them a collection of certainties: what they could look forward to (heaven), what they should fear (hell), what they could learn (lessons from the scriptures), and what they should do (practice charity and the other virtues of the saints). Sermons further explained each of the subjects represented to the worshippers. Artists were also called upon simply to decorate places of worship; the work was often paid for by individual donations.

Why did they paint the Madonna and Child so often?
The Madonna and Child are omnipresent because that image is doubly significant. A painting of the Madonna and Child represents more than just a mother and her baby. It is also meant to remind viewers that Jesus is the incarnation of the Word of God. The Virgin Mary symbolizes the institution of the Church and is the mother of all believers. Over the centuries artists have highlighted her humanity and tenderness, and she has become one of the most popular subjects in Christian art.

And why are there so many paintings of Christ on the cross?

The Christian faith rests on the belief in the resurrection of Christ. Crucifixion was a form of execution originally reserved for slaves and traitors, but Jesus' death turned the cross into a symbol of sacrifice and victory over death, a beginning instead of an ending. It was only natural for the Church to make sure that there were many images of it. Starting in the fifteenth century, increased knowledge of anatomy meant that the representations of Jesus became more realistic. Images of Christ also began to convey an ideal of physical beauty as well as spiritual perfection.

Why did artists paint the Annunciation so often?

The Annunciation is the moment when the Angel Gabriel comes to announce to Mary that she will give birth to the Son of God. It is also the moment when the Word of God becomes incarnate inside her. So the Annunciation scene is the meeting of the Word and the flesh, between spirit and matter. A fundamental part of the Christian message, it presented a challenge to painters: how to represent something that symbolizes the very process of creation (1).

Why does the baby Jesus often look like an adult?

Contrary to what people often think, it's not because of a lack of skill on the part of the painters, their inability to paint "real" babies. Jesus' facial features and expression needed to show the superior knowledge conferred on him by his dual nature: He is both human and divine, so he is represented as the size of a baby but with the maturity of an adult. Depending on the era, he is also shown, despite his small size, as an ancient orator in a toga with one hand raised (an image of the holy Word) or as an athlete (showing victory over evil). Generally he appears more robust and serious in the work of the Italian painters than in that of the Belgian artists, who showed him with a softer expression, smiling.

Why do people have golden circles around their heads?

The golden circle, a halo, symbolizes the light of God and is attached to divine beings or to saints. Halos are shown in different styles: as full circles or as a fine golden ring. Most of the time they follow the angle of the head, like a hat, but in paintings of the Middle Ages they remain parallel to the ground whatever the angle of the wearer's head (1). The halo is a symbol evoking the unchanging perfection of God (1).

Why are there sometimes portraits within religious paintings?

Portraits integrated in religious compositions usually represent those who commissioned the painting: they are portraits of the clients. In some cases the clients are included in the scene as additional characters: the Medici family in fifteenth-century Florence, for instance, had themselves painted as the Magi. In other paintings they mingle with the sacred protagonists of the scene but remain clearly distinguishable from them by their contemporary clothing and by being shown at prayer; in triptychs they are shown on side panels (sometimes even on the outside of the panels). It was a way for the clients to highlight their piety while also having their image preserved for posterity. In some religious pictures you can also see a self-portrait of the artist, which underlines his personal link with the subject matter.

Do people still paint religious paintings?

Religious paintings are produced much less often, reflecting the reduction of the role religion has played in Western society since the nineteenth century. But there have been many artists who give their interpretations of religious subjects, even if they have not devoted themselves exclusively to them. One interesting link between painting and spiritual matters lies in the growing popularity of abstract art. Numerous contemporary painters create works (including paintings, stained-glass windows, and installations) on commission for religious buildings. Without using literal illustration they approach the unknowable, indescribable absolute through the skillful combination of materials, colors, and light.

Why are there no paintings in synagogues or mosques?

Judaism and Islam are religions without images. They adhere scrupulously to the third commandment in the Old Testament: "You shall not make for yourself a graven image or any likeness of anything that is in heaven above." This commandment was designed to rule out any possibility of idolatry—to prevent men from worshipping painted or sculpted images of God rather than God himself. Although there are no figural paintings to be found in synagogues and mosques, there is much decorative art and symbolism. In Christian history the issue has been raised at several points and given rise to violent confrontations between factions: those for images and those against them. The Church finally pronounced in their favor, conscious of their educational power. Nevertheless, during the Reformation in northern Europe in the sixteenth century images were banned from places of worship.

What sources are scenes in religious paintings taken from?

Paintings of religious subjects refer not only to the Bible but also to two other key sources: the Apocrypha and *The Golden Legend*. Some people say that it is imperative to consult these three texts if you are to understand the many characters, situations, places, and symbols described by paintings.

- The Christian Bible is composed of the Old Testament and the New Testament. The Old Testament deals with themes linked to the creation of the world and of humanity, original sin, and the story of the Hebrews, the kings (10 and 14), and the prophets. The New Testament reports the life of Christ (the four gospels, 1), episodes in the lives of the apostles, and the Apocalypse.
- The books of the Apocrypha do not belong to the biblical texts but the Church allowed painters to use them for inspiration. Dating to the second, third, and fourth centuries, these stories inspired much of the iconography used in representing episodes in the lives of Christ and the Virgin Mary that are not included in the gospels; they are generally more sentimental in nature.
- *The Golden Legend* is a collection of stories, somewhere between history and legend, compiled and rewritten between 1225 and 1298 by Jacobus de Voragine, Archbishop of Genoa. It contains stories of a large number of saints (3) and their martyrdom.
- Religious theater also influenced painting by providing ideas for scenery, decor, or anecdotal detail. The public, used to seeing plays on the streets or on church steps, recognized familiar elements when they appeared in paintings.

Portraits

What is a portrait?

A portrait is a painting of a person, painted in such a way that the individual is recognizable. When history does not record the name of the model, but we know that at the time when it was painted the subject was identifiable, the picture is given a general title such as *Portrait of a Man* or *Portrait of a Young Woman*. The title can sometimes be a little more explicit when the painting contains particular details: for example, *Portrait of a Musician* or *Portrait of a Hunter*.

Who has their portrait painted?

Since the Middle Ages kings and queens have had their portraits painted either for themselves or for other royal family members. Having a portrait painted was a way of displaying political or religious power. During the Renaissance in the fifteenth century, wealthy people such as bankers and merchants would also have their portraits painted. Beginning in the seventeenth century and gaining prominence in the nineteenth century, members of the middle class began having their portraits painted—as long as they had enough money to pay the artist.

Does the painter choose whose portrait he paints?

In the past, when artists were in the service of royalty, they didn't have any choice: their position obliged them to paint what was demanded of them. These days artists are free to accept or refuse any commission. Near the end of the nineteenth century, artists began working less and less often for commission and instead independently produced paintings of their friends or people who interested them or whom they admired (20 and 29).

Why are people sometimes painted in profile?

The profile style was very popular in Italy in the fourteenth and fifteenth centuries and was inspired by ancient medals and coins. By adopting the pose of many Roman emperors, the person being painted emphasized his authority and nobility. The profile focused attention on the outline of the face without distracting the viewer with any particular expression. A portrait in profile highlights the enduring dignity of the subject. It is still popular today.

Why are faces often seen in three-quarter view?

In Byzantine churches the only face represented in a full-frontal view is that of Christ. Facing front in that way is an expression of divine power. A few rare portraits that do show a person's whole face are making an association between the model and God and eternity.

Unlike frontal views or profiles—which both suggest power and permanence—the three-quarter view is better suited to illustrating the transitory nature of man. It allows the artist to play with nuances of expression. Dutch painters adopted this method around the beginning of the fifteenth century, and it soon became prevalent.

What is the difference between a bust-length portrait and a half-length portrait?

A bust-length portrait shows a person from the shoulders up; the hands are not visible. Medieval and Renaissance portraits in profile or three-quarter view are always bust-length, following the tradition of ancient sculpture. From the sixteenth century onward it became more common to show subjects in half-length portraits—that is, just to their waist. In this kind of treatment, the hands provide an additional means of expression for the artist: are the hands visible or hidden (partially or entirely), fidgeting or at rest? These artistic decisions emphasize and add nuance to the psychological state of the model (6).

What is a full-length portrait?

A full-length portrait shows the subject standing up. Portraits of this kind were developed in the sixteenth century. Such a pose is particularly aristocratic or even regal, underlining the social standing of the person. A full-length portrait also provided an opportunity for the artist to reproduce clothing and environment. From the nineteenth century onward, this style of composition became very popular and was considered the height of elegance.

What is a state portrait?

The primary goal of the state portrait (generally an official portrait) is to highlight the social position of the individual and the power he holds. The extreme luxury of the clothes, the elegance of the pose, and the sumptuousness of the surroundings are key features: they highlight the importance of the title or role of the subject. Royal and court paintings create a spectacular impression. Equestrian portraits, inspired by Roman statues of emperors mounted on horseback, constitute a specific category of this type of portrait. They present the subject at the height of his powers, capable of political and military domination, both real and symbolic.

What is a self-portrait?

In a self-portrait the artist paints him- or herself with the help of a mirror (or, eventually, a photograph). Self-portraits can either stand alone as pieces of art or they can be incorporated into larger works (22) in which the artist appears among other figures. Sometimes artists depict themselves working, paintbrush in hand, but they might not necessarily make any reference to their profession.

How did people paint group portraits?

There are several types of group portraits: family portraits, portraits of members of a company or brotherhood, and groups of people bound by a particular circumstance. Often the subjects would pose together once, for the artist to get a sense of the positioning, and separately once, for the artist to capture their faces. For some portraits the subjects were never actually assembled at the same time, and the artist simply had to imagine the gathering for the purposes of the painting. Painting a group portrait challenged the artist to bring energy to the composition while giving the appropriate level of visual importance to each of the subjects.

Were portraits always a good likeness?

In the past the quality of the likeness was a critical factor; it is much less important in twentieth-century painting. After the advent of photography in the nineteenth century, the need for a perfect likeness diminished, and it became more important to capture the subject's character than exactly what he or she looked like. Another consideration for the artist in the past was the obligation to flatter the subject and show him or her in the best possible light.

Does the subject have to be there every time the artist paints?

No. Sometimes the subject was too important or too busy to spend a long time sitting. The artist made sure that a session with the subject was as short as possible. Sometimes she consulted another portrait of the subject when painting the face and then painted the body, the clothes, and the surroundings with the help of professional models or colleagues who would sit for her. In the twentieth century many artists preferred to work without a live model—some found the model's presence intimidating or restrictive—and worked from memory or from photos, This left them free to remember certain important features and to give a more subjective interpretation (29).

What is a portrait for?

A portrait provides a record of someone's appearance at a particular moment in his life. Before photography it was the only means, apart from sculpture, of doing so. A portrait could also provide information that was difficult to come by otherwise: a king looking for a wife often requested the portrait of a prospective bride whom he had not yet met. A painting provided an alternative to an absent person. That primary role of the portrait was evoked in an ancient legend in which a young woman paints the shadow of her lover on a wall as he leaves her, and in so doing discovers the art of painting and portraiture.

Has photography replaced the painted portrait?

It has in many ways because it has democratized pictures and allowed them to be reproduced in significant numbers. Nevertheless many portraits are still painted today. A portrait contains a quality of "presence" and a symbolic value, which are perhaps all the more important because a portrait is no longer the only means of capturing reality. A portrait is a conscious aesthetic choice on the part of the artist as much as on that of the subject.

Mythology, history, and allegory

What are mythological paintings about?

They represent scenes showing the exploits of gods, heroes, and other characters from Greek and Roman mythology. The ancient legends relate their exploits, their loves, and also their most ferocious quarrels. They gave artists the chance to deal with all sorts of human behavior elevated to the absolute: tenderness, jealousy, cruelty, courage, and vengeance (12).

Why are there many nudes in mythological paintings?

The nudity of mythological characters is linked to their superhuman nature. They represent ideas more than real people so they don't need to protect their bodies with clothing. Their perfect physiques also act as reference models; they have been rendered according to the ideals of physical beauty often found in ancient sculpture.

Who poses as nudes?

Both male and female professional models are used in art school classes and by working painters. It has become natural for artists to use people close to them, particularly in the twentieth century. In the past ancient sculptures provided great inspiration and served as a reference for correcting an "imperfection" in a real-life model. From the middle of the nineteenth century innovative artists such as Manet and sculptors such as Rodin started to use amateur models, because they liked their character and spontaneity.

Are all nudes mythological?

No, not all pictures of nudes have their inspiration in mythology. In religious painting, Adam and Eve, Jesus on the Cross, and various martyrs including St. Sebastian are usually represented naked. However, from the fifteenth century onward, these images were significantly influenced by representations of the gods of mythology: the appearance of Jesus, for example, owes a great deal to various statues of Apollo. Starting in the nineteenth century, artists began to feel bold enough to include nudes in non-religious paintings. So oriental themes began to appear, inspired by harem scenes, as a pretext for erotic evocations. In 1836 the French painter Edouard Manet created a scandal with his painting *Le Déjeuner sur l'herbe* (now in the Musée d'Orsay in Paris) because he gave up any pretence and simply presented a naked woman, her hat and clothes next to her, seated with two fully clothed gentlemen while another female figure bathes in the background. It was the first "contemporary" nude.

Why did people paint Venus so often?

Venus is the goddess of beauty and love and represents the perfect human body—a challenge for an artist to paint. Many paintings of Venus show her at the moment of her birth either emerging from the water (4) or lying down, sometimes asleep. Artists have also depicted her as more or less voluptuous; at the same time, her form has allowed artists to display their mastery of anatomy.

Why did people paint mythological subjects?

Mythological subjects gave artists the chance to paint nudes, an opportunity which had been denied them when painting most religious subjects. In Italy in the fifteenth century, at the time of the Renaissance, they became more prevalent. The observation of Greek and Roman sculpture, the study of anatomy, and a growing interest in ancient texts encouraged the proliferation of mythological images. No longer was painting limited to religious subjects and portraiture, painting began to enlarge its repertoire. Mythological characters were also used to symbolize and underline particular qualities of contemporary individuals. For example Louis XIV of France (nicknamed the Sun King) was linked in many sixteenth-century paintings to Apollo, the sun god.

From what sources did artists take their inspiration for mythological subjects?

There are many sources from Greek and Roman mythology. These include (in Greek) *The Iliad* and *The Odyssey* by Homer, and *Theogony* and *Works and Days* by Hesiod; and (in Latin) *The Aeneid, The Bucolics,* and *The Georgics* by Virgil, and *The Metamorphoses* by Ovid.

Many paintings are called an "allegory" of something. What does that mean?

The word *allegory* comes from the Greek *allegorein,* meaning "to speak in figures." In painting, allegory allows an artist to depict abstract ideas by presenting them as people or things. For example, the concept of time is often represented by an old man (time ages us), with wings (time flies), with a scythe (he cuts down life), or with an hourglass in his hand (time slips by). In some pictures, he pulls back his clothes to reveal the body of a young woman; this illustrates the idea that time reveals the truth. Allegory was often used to teach moral lessons of vice and virtue and to depict the richness of learning or of the arts (geometry, grammar, music, etc.). For example, justice is depicted as a woman holding scales and envy is a grimacing old woman. Death is shown as a skeleton holding a scythe.

What are historical paintings about?

Historical paintings can depict scenes either from ancient history or from the era in which the painter lived. The ancient world and the Middle Ages stimulated the imagination of artists offering them the chance to paint heroic or moving scenes. Contemporary historical themes, traditionally produced to official commission, commemorated events such as coronations, victories, or royal marriages. A great change took place in the nineteenth century when certain artists started to illustrate historical moments completely lacking in any glory. When artists started to observe life in this way, painting was enriched: it had a new role in creating a link with what was going on in society and the politics of the time and could be critical, provocative, or satirical (16).

Landscapes

What is a landscape?

A landscape is a representation of nature. Throughout the history of painting, landscapes have taken many different forms, depending on what the artist wanted to present—sweeping vistas or precise details. A landscape can be real or imaginary, countryside or seaside or even a town. Landscapes can also be combined with all other types of subjects.

Have people always painted landscapes?

During the second half of the thirteenth century, paintings began to include elements of nature (a tree or a mountain, for example). These elements weren't intended to be descriptive but were included as scenery for the person or the story in the painting. Eventually whole landscape backdrops started to appear behind religious scenes. By the fourteenth century, nature had so conclusively invaded religious painting that some pictures contained only tiny figures among vast natural scenery (7). From the seventeenth century onward the art of the landscape proper started to develop. Instead of acting as the background for other subjects, the landscape itself became the main subject. Particularly in the nineteenth century, landscapes included more motifs from daily life.

Does a landscape always depict a real place, as a photograph does?

From the fifteenth century onward, some landscapes contained identifiable elements of a particular place or region. But they didn't do so as a matter of course. It was more common to combine a number of elements from different places, real or imaginary. The artist edited nature, creating a final version that was totally idealized. Landscapes faithfully capturing real places, however, date back to seventeenth-century Holland. They grew in popularity throughout Europe in the nineteenth century; for example, in an Impressionist landscape you can recognize a particular bridge or cliff or country road.

Why did artists paint so many landscapes?

Landscape painting had several functions. First, a landscape is a way of celebrating divine creation; every blade of grass is a reflection of God and travel can represent a person's journey through life on earth (7). A landscape also served to capture historical reality. Holland in the seventeenth century, for example, had just won its political and religious independence, and Dutch artists produced a large number of landscapes that acted as a kind of inventory of the territory. Later, Romantic painters saw nature as a reflection of their souls and the relation between humans and the universe. Finally, Impressionist landscapes restored a sense of everyday life to landscapes, by including the smallest of changes: a ray of sunshine, a gust of wind, a snowy morning.

Is a landscape painted indoors or outdoors?

In the past, when landscapes weren't exact representations of one specific location, after making a number of studies from nature, painters worked in their studios. They composed their paintings with elements borrowed from different places to show the many different aspects of nature. As a result a landscape was an idealized summary of the world, a setting for a story. In the second half of the nineteenth century, artists began to paint their landscapes in the open air (19), made possible by the invention of paint in portable tubes. These paintings are also testimony to the changing social mores of the time: people went out more, they took trains, they went to the seaside. Painting in the open air had a huge impact on both the subject matter and the general aesthetic of paintings. The paintings started to focus on showing real things (as opposed to mythical creatures or holy individuals), things that everyone could see anywhere and at any time in the real world. Working in daylight also encouraged artists to lighten their color palettes and because of constant changes in the weather, they captured fleeting moments, using sketch-style techniques.

Scenes from everyday life and paintings of objects

Are there many paintings of everyday life?

Scenes from everyday life became increasingly popular in the sixteenth century and took their inspiration from every level of society. These paintings did not require viewers to be well read or well cultured because they did not deal with "noble" subjects such as Bible stories or ancient legends. As such they were considered to be of minor importance for a long time. But they sold better than paintings full of complex meanings, so more of these sorts of painting were produced (15). It was not until the nineteenth century that the term *genre painting* was coined.

What is a painting of objects called?

Different countries use different names. In France the term *nature morte* has been used since the eighteenth century to describe inanimate objects: game; hunting or fishing trophies; and flowers, fruit, or other objects. English speakers use the term "still life" (and Germans *Stilleben*), to differentiate "dead nature" from "tranquil nature." As with landscapes, still lifes began to be considered as subjects in their own right during the seventeenth century. Though objects had, of course, appeared in earlier paintings, they had always been elements in larger compositions and had never been the main subject before.

Does a still life show luxury objects?

No, in many cases still lifes show humble or even rustic objects chosen for the beauty of their shape, texture, or color. They can suggest the simplest of daily activities and gestures and evoke a close link with their owners (who do not appear in the painting).

Some still life paintings are called *vanitas*. What does that mean?

Vanitas is the Latin word for emptiness. Vanitas still lifes emphasize the brevity of life and the meaninglessness of material possessions. They can include objects that emphasize death (a skull) and/or the flight of time (an hourglass). They may also include an abundance of objects that will sooner or later crumble and decay. Vanitas paintings can appear very austere or act as a warning against the temptations of luxury.

Why do some still lifes show flowers, fruit, and vegetables that aren't in season at the same time?

Painters worked from nature but used numerous other sources to complete their paintings, including botanical reference books that gave them year-round access to a wider range of plants than nature has in any one season. Combining objects in one painting that never exist together in nature provided painters a means of creating a perfect picture—even more complete than everyday reality. With a single bouquet or plate of fruit suggesting the entire cycle of the seasons, for example, a painting could represent a whole year.

Do all still lifes have symbolic meanings?

Although the earliest still lifes were symbolic, not all paintings of this type hold such meaning. As with other types of paintings (landscapes and portraits), still lifes first appeared in religious paintings. When the objects themselves started to be painted independently, artists continued to imbue them with significance beyond their simple appearance: in a seventeenth-century painting (13) a bunch of grapes is a reference to Christ (the true vine, wine being linked to blood spilled on the Cross and present in communion). From the eighteenth century onward, objects became detached from their traditional symbolic meanings. In contemporary painting even if painters choose objects for their symbolic resonance they are no longer obliged to paint in code.

The price of a painting

Auction prices vary depending on the rarity of the painting and according to the period of the artist's career to which it belongs. Here are some examples of prices reached in recent auctions.

Old Masters and modern paintings
- *Venus and Adonis* by Titian (1488/1490–1576), 1555:
  about $13.3 million (€11 million) in 1991 at Christie's in London
- *The Massacre of the Innocents* by Reubens (1577–1640), about 1610:
  $76 million (about €62 million)in July 2002 at Christie's in London
- *Portrait of a Lady*, aged 62 by Rembrandt (1606–69), 1632:
  $35 million (about €28 million) in 2000 at Christie's in London
- *The Moulin de la Galette* by Pierre-Auguste Renoir (1841–1919), 1876:
  $78.1 million (about €64 million) in 1990 at Sotheby's in New York
- *Waterlily Pond with Path* by Claude Monet (1840–1926), 1900:
  $33 million (about €27 million) in 1999 at Sotheby's in London
- *Portrait of Doctor Gachet* by van Gogh (1853–90), 1890:
  $82.5 million (about €67 million) in 1990 at Christie's in New York

Contemporary paintings
- *Untitled* by Jean-Michel Basquiat (1960–88), 1981: $323,200
  (about €248,000) in November 2001 at Christie's in New York
- *IKB 86* by Yves Klein (1928–62), 1959: $780,003 (about €634,845)
  in February 2002 at Christie's in London
- *Man in Blue VII* by Francis Bacon (1909–92), 1954:
  $1,000,759 (about €814,575) in February 2002 at Christie's in London
- *Portrait of Man with Glasses* IV by Francis Bacon (1909–92), 1963: $1,265,177
  (about €1,029,711) in February 2002 at Christie's in London

Why are some paintings so expensive?

The exceptional is prized in painting, whether that is the artist's technical expertise or her intellect, because it offers a glimpse into an unknown world. The function of painting is much more than simply to reproduce images that already exist. Painting should touch your emotions and your senses that would otherwise have been unaffected—as it does in the work of van Gogh (21), Picasso (25), and Jean-Michel Basquiat (28).

A painting's symbolic value rests on the uniqueness of the work. Of course, the price of paintings, like that of any other product, is subject to market fluctuations. Paintings become more expensive after the death of the painter because the supply is limited—you can continue to find diamonds in a mine, but Francis Bacon is no longer around to produce more paintings. Though some artists make a lot of money, they are still in the minority (especially in comparison to actors and athletes).

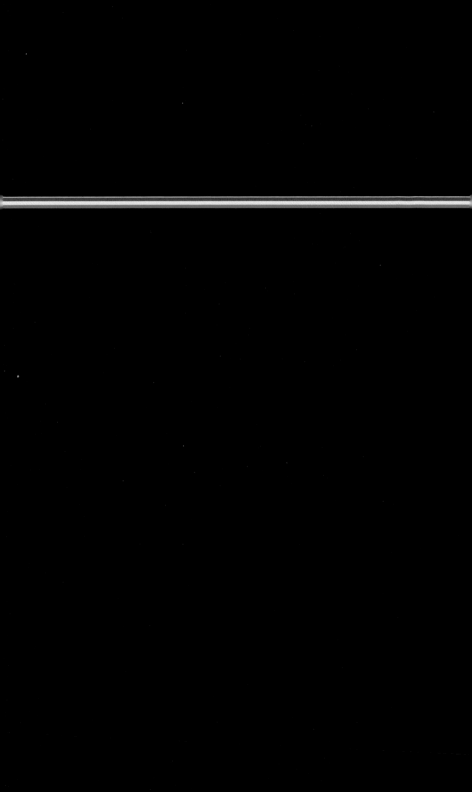

HOW TO LOOK AT
A PICTURE

The following pages aim to help you help children look at pictures. They offer a kind of user's manual to help you better appreciate any painting, no matter what it portrays, who it is by, or when it was painted. The pictures are explained step-by-step and the commentary roughly corresponds to a child's curiosity according to her age.

The framework is not rigid. The questions and comments can actually apply to either a child or an adult. You can read them all or choose a few (each paragraph stands alone and can be used independently). Or you can use the questions as inspiration to invent your own. The important thing is to learn to trust your own eyes.

The book does not attempt to include all the best-known paintings. The works here have been chosen to give a basis for better understanding of a wide spectrum of paintings, dating from the Middle Ages to the present day. They are all important works in the history of art. They can be seen in museums around the world or as reproductions in many other art books as well.

Red: five to seven years

A great way to begin is to simply identify what you see in the painting. This is not always straightforward, even for an adult. Identify the various elements of a painting; try not to look at it only as a cohesive whole.

Yellow: eight to ten years

Slightly more searching questions lead to a deeper understanding of the painting and require some thought and additional time.

Blue: eleven to thirteen and beyond

Consider the painting in relation to the outside world. The motivations of the painter are described as well as the historical importance of the work.

1 The Annunciation

Painted between 1430 and 1432; tempera on wood; 194 x 194 cm
Prado Museum, Madrid, Spain
Fra Angelico (Guido di Pietro, Fra Giovanni da Fiesole, known as Fra Angelico)
Born in Vicchio di Mugello, about 1400; died in Rome in 1455

There's an angel bowing before a young woman.

The angel Gabriel has come to tell Mary that she is going to have a baby. He's explaining that the baby will be the son of God and that he will be called Jesus. He is greeting her with respect, with his hands crossed on his chest, and though she remains seated, she is making the same gesture, bowing slightly. This scene, which is described in the Gospel according to Luke in the New Testament, is called the Annunciation.

Why doesn't Mary look amazed to see an angel in front of her?

In fact, we are the only ones who see the angel. The painter has shown the angel to make the "story" clearer, but within the world of the painting, Mary cannot see him: she only hears him. Other painters have shown her with a surprised or even a scared expression, but Fra Angelico preferred to focus on her serenity. She is calm, listening carefully to what the angel has come to tell her.

Who are the people in the garden?

They're Adam and Eve. The painting is actually telling two stories: the Annunciation and the Old Testament story of Adam and Eve being expelled from the Garden of Eden. Adam and Eve were punished for disobeying God and eating the fruit of the Tree of Knowledge. The angel in pink above their heads is making sure that they leave.

The angel and Mary both have pink robes and blond hair.

They are shown in the same colors because they are in harmony with each other. They understand each other perfectly. Their hair is as shiny as the sun, and their cheeks are pink, too. It's a very soft color, like the skin of the baby who will soon be born.

Will the angel stay with Mary?

No. The angel has only come to deliver a message. Even so, he doesn't quite come into the house: he stays in the doorway, like a guest who doesn't want to impose. His wings and his right foot are outside the pillar: he is between two worlds. He belongs to heaven, so he can only ever be a visitor on earth. His visit lasts just a few seconds.

The angel's mouth is shut; you can't see him speaking.

That is because Mary isn't listening to him with her ears. She simply understands his message. Gabriel is God's messenger; even though he greets Mary with words, he speaks directly to her soul.

Why is there a ray of sunlight crossing the picture?

The ray of sun represents the Word of God, coming to Mary. It travels through space like a laser beam. The painting shows the moment when the Word, entering Mary, takes the form of the baby that is to grow inside her.

Does the story take place at Mary's house?

Yes, the story takes place at Mary's house, but the house shown here doesn't look like the kind of house the historical Mary would have lived in, in Nazareth. The house here is much finer and much more elegant, more like the modern buildings of Italy in the fifteenth century, when Fra Angelico was working. He used the house like a stage set to focus attention on a crucial element of the story: while Mary is at home indoors, the angel enters.

There is another room in the background.

That room helps you to imagine the rest of the house. By showing the plain wooden furniture and the bench with the sun on it, Fra Angelico makes it clear that Mary's house was very simple. He only painted part of the other room; the rest remains unseen. The painting tells a story, but it also suggests that it is impossible to understand everything. It depicts a mystery.

There is a little black-and-white bird perched on the iron bar.

That's a swallow. Its role in the painting is to show the season during which the story takes place. Each spring these birds return home from the warm countries where they have spent the winter. The presence of a swallow here shows that it is spring: the Annunciation is supposed to have taken place on March 25 (nine months before Jesus was born on December 25).

Why is there a white bird flying above the angel's head?

That's a dove, representing the Holy Spirit. The dove shows that the Angel Gabriel's message is holy. While the swallow indicates a specific time of year, the dove symbolizes eternity.

Is God anywhere in the picture?

God appears in the painting in two different places. It is his face that is slightly turned toward the angel in the carved disk between the two arches. The two hands in a circle of light at the top of the painting are also his; they are accompanying the messenger as he speaks to Mary.

What is in the little paintings at the bottom?

The little paintings show other scenes from Mary's life. This part of the painting is known as a predelle; it's almost like a comic strip at the bottom of the main panel. The painter shows certain famous scenes from Mary's life: birth, marriage, the Visitation (she visits her cousin Elizabeth, who was herself pregnant with John the Baptist), the Adoration of the Magi, the presentation of Jesus at the temple, and the Dormition of the Virgin (her death). The frame that surrounds the whole has not been changed since this altar painting was completed, which is rare.

Why does Mary have a book in her lap?

It looks as if she has been interrupted reading. This isn't exactly historically accurate. Mary probably couldn't read, and, during that time period, text was written on large scrolls, not in books. The reading imagery reminds us, however, that the prophet Isaiah announced in the Old Testament the birth of a child who would be a sign from God. Christians believe that the child was Jesus. The book Mary is holding highlights the link between the ancient prophecy and the Annunciation.

What's the connection between the Annunciation and Adam and Eve?

The two episodes did not happen at the same time or in the same place, but they are linked by their meanings. Adam and Eve represent original sin and disobedience to God. On the other hand, because of the Annunciation, Mary embodies the idea of submission to God's will. Placing the two themes so closely together highlights the story of Jesus, who will redeem the sins of the world. In this way, it's like the painting consists of two acts: Adam and Eve, small on the left-hand side, are about to leave the picture, while, on the other side, the angel and the light are entering a clear beautiful place. What is lost on one side is offered to the other.

Why did Fra Angelico give so much emphasis to architecture?

Architecture symbolizes the concept of building. Here the double arches in the shape of Mary's initial, M, help us interpret the painting: Mary is being compared to a temple. She is a holy place where the unborn child will grow. The painting shows the exact moment where the story begins: on the marble floor, the colors of sky, light, and nature (blue, yellow, and green) mingle together. When the angel arrives, it is as though these colors have been blown toward Mary by a strong wind. They symbolize the new life being breathed into her.

₂ The Arnolfini Portrait

Painted in 1434; oil on wood; 82 x 60 cm
National Gallery, London, England
Jan van Eyck
Born about 1390–1400; died in Bruges, Belgium, 1441

They're a couple.
Yes, Giovanni and Giovanna Arnolfini are shown holding each other's hands and looking at one another. They are both Italian but live in Flanders, far from home. It's there, in the city of Bruges, that they had this portrait painted.

They've got a little dog.
The little dog is standing between them, at their feet, as if he's standing right in front of the painter. The dog looks as calm as his owners. He is turned toward the woman; perhaps he is used to being by her side.

Is the woman expecting a baby?
Probably not. The artist must have shown her with a rounded stomach because in the fifteenth century, a rounded shape was the fashion. Some women even wore little cushions under their clothes.

They are wearing winter clothes.
The velvet clothes with fur linings (called pelisses) show that the Arnolfinis must have been rich. Houses were often cold, particularly in the Low Countries of the Netherlands where they lived. The man is wearing his hat, which suggests that he has either just come in or that he is on his way out.

What room are they in?
Even though there is a large four-poster bed on the right side of the picture, the room is not necessarily a bedroom. In elegant households fancy beds were used to decorate the most beautiful rooms, but no one ever slept in them. The Arnolfinis are probably standing in the room where they usually received their guests.

There are shoes on the ground.
The clogs in the bottom corner of the painting are large enough to belong to Mr. Arnolfini. People wore them over their shoes to keep their shoes clean: at that time there were no pavements and roads were often full of mud and garbage. Giovanni would have left them there, close to the door. The small red mules in the background are light slip-on shoes that Giovanna wore indoors.

♦ ♦ ♦

There is some fruit near the window.
The fruit provides a warm note in an otherwise dark part of the painting. Oranges, which were imported from Spain, were very expensive. Too bitter to eat, they were used to perfume the house. It is possible that the apple on the windowsill is a reminder of the Garden of Eden (representing the fruit of the Tree of Knowledge).

There is a mirror on the far wall.

It's a convex mirror, made from a bubble of blown glass. The reflective surface was obtained by adding lead. This kind of convex, or "fish-eye," mirror not only reflects objects in front of it but also objects to the sides, which is why you can see the reflection of the window. We can also see the Arnolfinis reflected from behind, and in front of them the image of two other people, one in blue and the other in red. Many people believe that they are the painter and his friend or assistant.

What is written underneath the mirror?

The artist's signature and the date appear as if they had been painted directly onto the wall in large and intricate lettering. The words are written, as was the custom at that time, in Latin, the language of learning. It says, "Johannes de eyck fuit hic. 1434," which means "Jan van Eyck was here. 1434." Artists usually inscribed their paintings with the words *fecit* (made) or *pinxit* (painted), but here the painter is emphasizing his presence in the scene instead of associating himself with the production of the painting.

What is that next to the mirror?

It's a rosary. Everyday rosaries are made of wood, but this is a precious one, made of crystal. Its placement there was a reminder not to neglect one's prayers, especially when admiring oneself in the mirror. The ten little enamels set in the mirror's frame depict scenes from the life of Jesus Christ and probably serve the same purpose. These pictures make it difficult for people looking in the mirror to get lost in vanity and forget their Christian duty.

Why is there a candle lit overhead when it is broad daylight?

We don't know for sure. Often a candle's flame symbolizes spiritual light. In that sense, the candle is just as useful in daylight as it is in darkness. Alternatively the candle may illustrate how natural light and spiritual light complement one another.

Why does Giovanni Arnolfini have his right hand raised?

Some historians think he is in the middle of making a vow, saying "I swear," during a ceremony to mark his engagement or marriage to Giovanna. (In that era people were legally allowed to hold such ceremonies in their own homes without any officials being present.) Others believe that the portrait shows them just after the marriage, which would mean he is welcoming his bride into the house.

Why aren't they smiling?

This must be a significant moment in their lives, and they want to preserve the memory of the day. Van Eyck shows them looking solemn to emphasize the occasion, whatever it was. The portrait shows them as serious people, conscious of their importance. From a technical perspective, the rigidity of their expressions also makes it easier for the painter to capture them accurately.

Who were the Arnolfinis?

Giovanni came from a wealthy family of fabric merchants, and he did much business with the court of the Duke of Burgundy. We know from various records, for example, that eleven years before the date of this painting, he sold Philippe le Bon a collection of tapestries that had originally been destined for the Pope. Giovanni enjoyed increasingly eminent positions and was even made chamberlain for the court. Giovanna also came from a large family of fabric and fur merchants. The Arnolfinis' social and financial position explains how they were able to commission Jan van Eyck, the Duke of Burgundy's personal artist.

Did other people have their portraits painted in the same style?

Having one's portrait painted full-length, so that the whole body was visible, was a completely new style at this time. It became more acceptable later on, but not for at least another seventy years. And, even then, for a long time the full-length style was reserved only for royalty or the aristocracy.

Did van Eyck invent oil painting?

No, oil painting had existed for several centuries before van Eyck started painting, but he did a great deal to perfect the art by taking full advantage of the technical advances of his time. The oil paint that was being made then dried a lot more swiftly than the oils that had existed previously. Van Eyck developed a process where he used several very fine layers of translucent paint, which allowed him to give his paintings such subtlety of light and color. It was no longer necessary to add white paint to a color to lighten it; van Eyck's technique allowed the color to retain its intensity. In the lighter areas of this painting, he shows an external light hitting the back wall; in the dark areas, the colors are more opaque. This very fluid style allowed for an extraordinary level of detail. The result is as bright and shiny as enamel.

Is it true that we don't really know what this painting is about?

There are many theories, and whole books have been written about this painting—still, many questions about it remain unanswered. What was the occasion for this unique picture to be painted? Why is the man holding up his hand? Is the little dog a pet, a symbol of faithfulness, or both? Why did the artist sign the picture in such a spectacular and unusual fashion? Who were the real models for this picture? With this work, van Eyck created one of history's most enigmatic paintings.

3 St. George and the Dragon

Painted in about 1455–60; oil on canvas; 56.5 x 74 cm
National Gallery, London, England
Paolo Uccello (Paolo di Dono, known as Uccello)
Born in Florence 1397; died in Florence 1475

What's happening in this painting?

It's the story of a knight fighting a dragon. The animal's blood has spilled onto the ground. The woman watching them is wearing a small crown, so she must be a queen or a princess.

Who is the young woman?

She is the dragon's prisoner; the knight has come to rescue her. She seems forced to the edge of the picture, taking up only a narrow space. The only other place in the picture for her to hide is in the cave, but maybe she's scared because it's so dark.

Where did the dragon come from?

He probably just came out of the cave behind him. It must be the entrance to his lair. Perhaps it's huge, filled with other terrifying creatures.

But dragons don't exist!

Yes, dragons are imaginary creatures, but they combine many of the nastiest features of other, real animals: a huge mouth with enormous teeth like a lion, feet with claws like a bear, wings like a bat, a tail curled up like a snake, and green skin like crocodiles. But they also breathe fire.

Why isn't the princess frightened?

The knight has come to rescue her, and she trusts him. Now she no longer has to be afraid. She is waiting patiently for the fight to be over. But notice that she already has the dragon on a leash as if it were a dog.

Will the knight win?

Definitely. He seems to have already seriously wounded the dragon. Also, the fact that he is riding a white horse indicates that he will win: the brightest of whites will overcome the dark shadows of the cave. Behind him the sky is spinning, as if he has a whole army of clouds at his command.

How does the story end?

It doesn't really end. St. George, the knight, has been sent by God to drive back the forces of evil. He has wounded the dragon, but the dragon doesn't die. Symbolically, the death of the dragon would mean that evil no longer exists on earth, which, in the Christian faith, is impossible. We can resist evil, get around it, run away from it, or even send it into submission, but we will never manage to get rid of it completely. There is no final victory over evil in life.

St. George only hits the dragon once.

The painting captures the moment when St. George strikes the decisive blow. He cannot hesitate. As a heavenly soldier he knows no doubt; he knows exactly what he has to do and how he must do it. He fulfils his mission perfectly.

The scene doesn't look very realistic.

The artist wasn't trying to paint reality. He wanted to tell a fairy-tale story. That's why the painting looks like a scene in a play, with the characters dressed up in medieval costumes. St. George doesn't look like a real warrior in combat; he's a noble knight in shining armor, handsome and clean. The princess looks totally serene, not at all hurt or frightened.

The cave is strange.

It looks a bit like the caves for monkeys or bears in the zoo. It almost looks like it's made of papier-mâché or cardboard. Caves and mountains were often painted in this style to resemble the model caves used for animals in carnivals, street performances, or sometimes even churches. This created a link between spectators' daily lives and the world shown in paintings.

The artist doesn't really show how the people are feeling.

The painting isn't about their feelings. It is true that the knight doesn't look particularly pleased with his victory over the dragon, and the princess looks neither afraid nor relieved. She is not expressing any gratitude to St. George. This is because the painting doesn't depict ordinary people suddenly plunged into an adventure; each character represents an idea. The knight represents good, and the dragon represents evil. Good and evil are in a constant battle over the souls of human beings, represented here by the princess.

The dragon is all twisted.

Unlike the princess who appears made of all vertical lines, the dragon's body juts out in all directions. His silhouette is irregular and pointy like the jagged edges of his cave. He is full of contradictions—he is at once a snake, a tiger, and a crocodile. You cannot trust any part of his appearance. The circles on his wings are red and blue on the outside (the princess's side), but on the inside (the knight's side) they are blue and white. They are like targets that change color depending on who is fighting. But don't forget that it's only in Western tradition that dragons are used to symbolize evil.

St. George is made of rounded shapes.

The knight and his steed are in harmony with one another. Nature is also at one with him: even the clouds roll themselves up over his head. You can almost hear the thunder in the air. Uccello has rendered St. George with a series of curves that suggest his concentration: the curves of the horse's neck and tail, the armor, and the clouds in the sky. These shapes create a sense of unity and momentum. St. George appears to move with perfect efficiency, like the planets in orbit.

It's daytime, but you can still see the moon.

The painting is all about contrast. The fight it depicts is not just any fight; it's a conflict between the absolute forces of good and evil. It takes place simultaneously during the day and during the night. The sky is blue, but, above the knight, we can see a small crescent moon. The laws of nature are turned on their heads: grass has grown in regularly shaped patches without covering all the stone. Rich soil lies next to barren earth, and the borders between them are sharply defined. To the left there is the weight of the rocks and, to the right, the weightlessness of the rolling clouds.

Did Uccello make up this story?

No, the story of St. George and the princess of Trebizonde has been painted by many artists. It's taken from *The Golden Legend,* written by Jacobus de Voragine in the thirteenth century, but the story was inspired by other, more ancient tales. Uccello actually painted two versions of this story; the other, with the dragon standing on its hind legs, is at the Musée Jacquemart-André in Paris. Such paintings weren't just meant to be pleasant to look at; they were intended to remind people that they could and should fight the devil to save their souls.

4 The Birth of Venus

Painted 1485; tempera on canvas; 184.5 x 285.5 cm
Uffizi Gallery, Florence, Italy
Botticelli (Sandro di Mariano Filipepi, known as Botticelli)
Born in Florence 1445; died in Florence 1510

She's completely naked!

Of course she is—she's just been born. The young woman next to her is about to help her get dressed. This is an unusual birth because it's the birth of a goddess. According to legend Venus was already an adult when she was born.

Where are her parents?

They're in the picture, but not in the form of people. Mythology says Venus's parents are the sea and the sky. She has just emerged from the sea, and the wind is making little foam-topped waves on the surface of the water. Venus is sometimes known as the woman born of the waves.

Why is she standing on a shell?

If she were swimming, we wouldn't be able to see her clearly, and the painter didn't want it to look like she is making an effort to get to shore. (Making an effort wouldn't be fitting for a goddess.) So, the painter gave her a kind of a boat. The shell is a beautiful and natural object, delicately shaped and colored. It's perfect for Venus, the goddess of beauty and love.

Who is the woman bringing her clothes?

She's one of the three Graces, Venus's traditional companions. There are innumerable flowers scattered all around her as well as on her dress because Venus was born in springtime. She is running lightly, on the tips of her toes, so she won't miss Venus's arrival. She is already lifting her arm so she can be ready to put the cloak over her shoulders.

Are the other two figures angels?

This isn't a Christian painting, so they're not really angels. They have wings because they live in the sky. The man is called Zephyr and the woman is Aura—they are the winds. They are gently blowing the goddess to the shore. The artist shows their breath with little wisps of white. Zephyr's breath is stronger than Aura's—it lifts Venus's hair and the large cloak held by the Grace.

♦ ♦ ♦

What kinds of flowers are shown in the painting?

Roses are in the air surrounding Venus. Roses always accompany her because they symbolize love and beauty. It is said that a rose bush sprang from the ground where she first stepped ashore. Because it's springtime, cornflowers also appear. On the Grace's dress there is myrtle, which stays green throughout the winter and is a symbol of immortality.

Why don't the winds have the same color skin?

Because the artist wanted to show two winds of different strength, he has shown them as a man and a woman. Traditionally male figures are painted with darker, more matte skin, as if it has been tanned by the sun. Women are usually shown with very light skin, as though they have always been protected from the sun, so that they seem gentler, more delicate and fragile.

Why is this shell known as a "coquille St. Jacques"?

In the Middle Ages, one of the most important Christian pilgrimages was to the sanctuary of St. James (Jacques) of Compostelle, in Spain. According to legend, St. James the Great (killed in Jerusalem in 44 C.E.) was buried there. It became customary for pilgrims, who subjected themselves to many weeks of walking, to gather shells from the seashore to prove that they hadn't given up along the way. That's where the name coquille St. Jacques comes from.

Venus has a dreamy expression.

She's not looking at anything in particular and her mind is elsewhere, as if she is remembering the faraway place she has come from. This dreamy expression is a hint to us from the painter: it's not enough to recognize how beautiful Venus is. We also have to understand that her beauty comes from another world, a world we cannot know or understand, where everything must be perfect, like she is.

The waves aren't very realistic.

Nature isn't the subject of the painting. The artist didn't need to paint a faithful reproduction of the sea. The little waves sit on the surface of the water; they don't look natural, but they do indicate movement.

Why is the goddess standing on only one leg?

This pose is called *contrapposto*. It gives a supple and flattering line to the leg and body that is much more elegant than if the model was standing with both feet flat on the ground. It was used in many ancient sculptures, and painters have often been inspired by it. Even today models in fashion shows and in publicity photographs stand like this, with their weight on one hip.

Venus is partly covering herself up with her hand and her hair.

Tradition demands that Venus is decent. Her gesture here is based on an ancient statue called *Venus Pudica* (in Latin, *pudica* means "chaste, virtuous, and modest"). She isn't covering up much more than a small bikini would. However, the movement of her arm brings her to life and allows the artist to put her hands in a realistic position. To achieve the same effect, in other paintings Venus is sometimes depicted lifting her wet hair.

Why is there hardly any shadow in the painting?

The whole painting was painted using light, gentle colors, to show Venus's extraordinary beauty. Her skin tone reminds us of pearls. She is radiant, and the painting shows a world transformed by that radiance. The right-hand side of the painting is a little darker, but the overall effect suggests that Venus will chase away the shadows.

Is Venus always shown naked?

She's almost always shown naked because she is a supernatural being. She cannot be scratched or harmed by the cold or any of the other things that affect humans. She is the goddess of beauty and must show her perfectly proportioned body. (It was very important for a painter to know how to accurately portray anatomy, and painting a nude provided an excuse to show one's expertise.) In Botticelli's time people thought that beauty, goodness, and truth were inseparable. The picture of Venus shows not only physical but also spiritual beauty.

The characters look as though they have been stuck onto the landscape.

This effect is created by the accentuated outlines around the figures. You can follow the dark line that contains each figure and seems to cut it out. The body, rigidly defined and contained in this way, appears like a prison for the soul, enclosing it until death. This idea was very popular in Florence in the fifteenth century. It was the product of neo-Platonic philosophers, who were close to the Medici family, who employed Botticelli. Botticelli often spent time with these philosophers, and his paintings were greatly influenced by their ideas. This might be one explanation for Venus's melancholy expression: it is only through her gaze that her spirit can escape from the body that contains it.

Is this painting very famous?

Yes, it's one of the most famous paintings in the history of art. It celebrates the fundamental idea of the appearance of beauty on the earth. But the painting means so much more than just the meaning conveyed by the subject; it is an homage to grace rendered in shapes so simple it gives the impression that everything is easy. It flows like a melody. Previously the only woman's body that artists painted in the nude was Eve's, in scenes where she is tempted by the serpent or expelled from Eden for disobeying God. Her nudity was associated with the shame of original sin. Here, for the first time, the opposite is true. Venus is luminous, and the image is full of her vitality. Botticelli invites viewers to consider the harmony of the mind and body.

5 The Temptation of St. Anthony

Painted about 1505–06; triptych, oil on wood; central panel 131.5 x 106 cm
Museu Nacional de Arte Antiga, Lisbon, Portugal
Hieronymus (Jerôme) Bosch
Born in Bois-le-Duc about 1453; died in Bois-le-Duc 1516

What story is the painting telling?

It tells the story of an episode in the life of St. Anthony, who lived in fourth-century Egypt. He decided to withdraw from the world, deprive himself of everything, and pray continuously. But his mind was troubled, and all sorts of thoughts kept him from concentrating. These thoughts tormented him constantly. The artist has represented them in the painting as dozens of little characters.

There are people everywhere!

Yes there are, and that's the problem it's trying to express. The picture shows what happens to a man who has gone into the desert to be alone but finds himself surrounded on all sides and not knowing where to turn for a moment of peace.

Where is St. Anthony?

He appears once on each of the three panels that compose this work. In the central panel, he is painted very small, right in the middle. He is kneeling, wearing blue clothes and a hood. His face is turned toward the viewer, perhaps to keep from looking at all the horrible creatures surrounding him.

The painting is full of monsters.

The painting is positively groaning with monsters put there to help the viewer understand what is going on in poor St. Anthony's mind. They appear in the water, on the land, in the sky, and even in the flames in the distance. It's impossible for St. Anthony to get away from them—they can walk, crawl, fly, swim, and breathe fire.

There's a lot of red in the painting.

The color red gives movement to the picture. The artist has used it in several areas to keep our eyes moving: to the left there is the big strawberry from which people are emerging; in the middle, at the bottom, there is a boat with a fish's head and a cape; on the right, you can see a mouselike creature wearing scarlet. In the distance there is an entire village going up in flames. All this red gives the painting a feeling of fear. Maybe St. Anthony has a fever and is delirious.

Why is the painting in three pieces?

This kind of picture is called a triptych. The central panel is twice as wide as the two others, which are actually shutters on hinges and can be shut, like a cupboard, hiding all three images. When it is closed the pictures are protected. Also, if the images are sometimes hidden and aren't constantly on display, there is a slight element of surprise each time it is opened again.

All the characters are strange.

They are terrifying because you don't know exactly what they are. It's impossible to name them or put them into any kind of category. In front of St. Anthony there is a man's head on top of a pair of legs, and behind him there's someone with a pig's snout. The creatures are made up of elements that don't go together, as though the painter has collected lots of random parts in order to create them.

The countryside in the background on the right is the only peaceful place.

In the distance everything looks peaceful, which tells us that as soon as St. Anthony has passed this terrible ordeal, his world—that is, his mind—will be at peace again. Even if all he encounters right now are obstacles, he is turned in the direction of peace. You could draw a straight line between his body and the horizon (passing through the little chapel where Christ is making the sign of the cross). The distant land is out of reach at the moment, but St. Anthony will make it there eventually.

Why is it so hard to find St. Anthony in the painting?

This painting shows the chaos in the saint's head. It isn't until later that we can actually find the saint. In this way the artist is depicting what the demons want to do: they want to take up all the space in Anthony's head and squeeze out the man himself. They almost manage to persuade him—and us—that they are all that exists. The painting is like a trap to be thwarted, a treasure hunt where the treasure is St. Anthony himself.

Your eyes are pulled in all directions.

Hieronymus Bosch did all he could to make the picture difficult to decipher. It's impossible to read it using the logic of a story: you start off looking at one figure, then you notice another, then a third, and perhaps you begin to panic and become confused. You probably even forgot where you started looking. The painting prevents you from creating a logical sequence of ideas. On the contrary, it makes you feel like the world is spinning around you, and it takes a supreme effort of will not to lose your mind, which is what St. Anthony is feeling, too.

Are Hieronymus Bosch's paintings the only ones with demons in them?

Many artists painted demons in their depictions of hell, but Bosch's demons are the most varied, complex, and surprising, and maybe are some of the funniest that have ever been seen. Perhaps one of the most striking things about Bosch's demons is that they aren't living in hell but are part of life on earth. However, this isn't just a fantasy on the part of the painter; it reflects sixteenth-century philosophies about the power of evil in the world. The demons are everywhere: they inhabit the four traditional elements (earth, air, fire, and water) throughout the painting.

Weren't people shocked by paintings like this?

Hieronymus Bosch painted for churches. He was a religious man, and well respected by his peers. After his death his greatest collector was Philippe II of Spain (1527–98), a fervent Catholic. Even though Bosch's paintings were outlandish, they also showed the hellish nature of temptation. Paintings like this were a sort of moral warning. However, it is also possible that his demon pictures were painted for small groups of fans and not widely seen. The painter had personal wealth that allowed him a certain amount of freedom to take on only the commissions that interested him.

Is Hieronymus Bosch a typical painter of his time?

His paintings, while certainly strange, were perfectly in tune with the ideas of his time. His work was always based on Christian thought, which dominated philosophy at the time, but the paintings also reflected the thinking of a very tumultuous period in history. At the beginning of the sixteenth century, the end of the world had been predicted for the year 1500, the Church was in a deep crisis that would eventually bring about the Reformation, and society at large was confused and disoriented.

Could you say that Hieronymus Bosch made surrealist paintings?

Technically speaking, Surrealism as an artistic movement was not born until after World War I. But it's clear that Bosch was a source of inspiration for twentieth-century artists who borrowed many of his tricks (inverting sign and signifier, making incongruous combinations, replacing hard with soft and solid with liquid, etc.). Though there are strong formal links between Bosch's paintings and modern art, that doesn't mean he was a surrealist ahead of his time. Rather, it means that the Surrealists, who used some of his stylistic innovations to express very different ideas, owe much of their inspiration to him.

6 The Mona Lisa

Painted about 1503–06; oil on wood; 77 x 53 cm
The Louvre Museum, Paris, France
Leonardo da Vinci (Leonardo di ser Piero da Vinci)
Born in Vinci, near Florence, 1452; died at Amboise, France, 1519

Who is this woman?

She lived in Italy about five hundred years ago. Her first name is Lisa, but she was called Mona Lisa, which means Lady Lisa. Her family name was "del Giocondo," so she is also known as *La Gioconda* (in Italy) or *La Joconde* (in France).

Who painted her?

The portrait is by Leonardo da Vinci. He was already very well known at the time. He lived in the same city as Lisa del Giocondo.

There aren't many colors.

Leonardo da Vinci did not use many different colors, and he especially didn't use many bright ones. He felt his paintings should be easy to look at. He wanted your eyes to take in one item at a time and then move smoothly across the canvas like a caress or a cloud.

Why is the painting so dark?

The picture was definitely lighter when it was first painted, but over the years it has aged. Instead of getting wrinkles, as people do, paintings crack and darken. The protective layer of varnish has also changed and taken on a brownish tint. Years ago, Mona Lisa certainly had paler skin and looked much healthier. The sky behind her was more blue, too.

It looks as though she doesn't have any hair.

She does have hair, but, in that era, the fashion was for women to have some of their hair removed, raising their hairline very high on the forehead and leaving their faces clearly visible. If she could see us today, she would probably be horrified by our different hairstyles. She'd think we look very scruffy.

Did Leonardo da Vinci paint her because he thought she was beautiful?

We don't know whether he thought she was particularly beautiful. He painted the portrait because Mona Lisa's husband commissioned him to paint it. It is likely that many people thought she was good-looking.

Why do people always say the Mona Lisa is beautiful?

It might be that people confuse the painting with the woman. Saying the painting is beautiful, for some people, is the same as saying the woman in the painting is beautiful. But they are two very different things: this is a picture of a woman, not the woman herself in flesh and blood. The painting is world famous, not the woman. When people talk about "Mona Lisa," we probably don't think of the woman, who she was, or where she lived. We think of the painting, of this portrait.

Why is this painting so famous?

It was the first time that a portrait had looked so lifelike. Instead of painting Mona Lisa with a fixed expression, as any other painter would have done, da Vinci gave her a fleeting look, a sort of half-smile that might be just starting or just finishing. And although everything around her is peaceful, the light too is in the process of changing. No one had ever seen a picture like this, able to give the impression of time passing.

What's in the background?

She is sitting in a *loggia*, a sort of balcony, and she is turned toward us, as if we are with the painter inside the house. Behind her we see the view that she would have been looking at: valleys, a river with a bridge, and roads leading into the distance. Although she is the only person in the painting, she is not cut off from the rest of the world.

Why didn't Leonardo da Vinci paint more accurately?

In real life not everything is clearly visible, especially small details in the distance. That's why he drew almost everything in the painting without hard edges or outlines. We can't really make out where one shape ends and the next begins; we imagine them more than we actually see them. They are lost in a kind of mist. The mountains in the background are so hazy that they merge into the sky. This painting technique was called *sfumato*, which comes from the Italian word *sfumare*, meaning to evaporate like smoke.

The hands are very well lit.

Her hands play an important role in this painting. Some people fiddle with their hands or drum their fingers or their hands tense up even when the rest of their body appears to be relaxed. Mona Lisa is absolutely peaceful and calm. We can tell this from her hands, which are gently resting on one another.

This isn't a very happy painting.

This painting gives a melancholy impression when compared to other paintings from the same period that are lighter and more colorful. In paintings of that era, light and dark were mainly used as symbols. Light colors represented good and shadows and dark colors represented evil. Artists painted as little shadow as possible. By giving equal importance to both light and shade, da Vinci was doing something new: he was treating his subject scientifically as much as he was treating it symbolically. Elements that are well lit can be seen, observed, and understood but elements that are in darkness remain unknown.

Did other artists paint in the same style as Leonardo da Vinci?

It can be argued that no one has ever been able to match Leonardo's famous *sfumato*. But, thanks to him, painters gradually started to give shadow a greater role. Artists also started to compose their portraits as he did, with the subject's body forming a large triangle like a pyramid. Think of the Egyptian pyramids: they were symbols of the sun, like rays of light made from stone that evoked the idea of eternity. In Mona Lisa's time the triangle composition was used in sacred paintings such as the Madonna and Child. By using this style in a portrait, da Vinci was going against tradition.

Was the painting famous in Leonardo's time?

Yes, it was very famous. Everything about it was new: the pyramid composition, the idea of showing the subject in a realistic environment, the way the subject is linked to the landscape, the use of light and shade (*chiaroscuro*), the sensation of capturing a moment in Mona Lisa's smile. These were not just technical innovations; they showed a new way of looking at the world. An average woman became a symbol of humanity, captured for eternity in one moment between a passing ray of light and a shadow that holds her secrets.

Did Leonardo paint many paintings?

Painting was just one of many subjects he was interested in; today we only know of about a dozen of his paintings. However, he left behind large quantities of drawings and notes that show how busy he was. He studied anatomy, geology, botany, astronomy, and optics. He was fascinated by the natural world and by anything to do with movement: the dust of a battle, the wind in a storm, the light at dusk, a grimace, or a smile. In addition to being a painter, he was also a sculptor, an architect, and an engineer. He invented flying machines and designed fortifications and weapons. Everything he did was an attempt to deepen his knowledge and understanding of the world around him. The Mona Lisa represented such an important stage in his learning that he kept the painting until he died. She never received her portrait. This painting not only captures the woman's image, it also perfectly illustrates Leonardo da Vinci's thinking.

₇ Landscape with St. Jerome

Painted about 1520; oil on wood; 74 x 91 cm
The Prado Museum, Madrid, Spain
Joachim Patenier
Born at Dinan or Bouvignes between 1475 and 1485, died at Antwerp 1524

This is a large landscape with small villages.

The countryside stretches as far as the eye can see. It's dotted with castles and villages full of small houses. There are mountains and forests, a light green lake on the right, and in the distance is the sea.

Who is the old man in the shelter?

The old man in the shelter is St. Jerome. He wants to be alone to think without being disturbed by anyone. He decides to leave city life behind and to live outdoors. He is very small in the painting. The way he's positioned in the corner like that, it conveys the idea that he wants to be left in peace.

He has an animal with him.

He is looking after a lion with a thorn in its paw. The grateful lion became his companion, like a dog. They are always shown together in paintings. The lion can actually be seen again in the painting, a little farther away on the right-hand side—he's bounding toward a donkey that is carrying a load of wood. The lion isn't going to eat the donkey; he's chasing after it because St. Jerome has entrusted him with the donkey's safety. The lion must take it to pasture and make sure it's protected from harm.

This painting contains mainly green, blue, and brown colors.

Green is the color of grass and trees, blue is the color of the sea and the sky, and brown is the color of earth and rocks. However, these three colors have not been used in a uniform way; each is full of subtleties. Patenier uses dozens of different hues, and, depending on where they are used, he creates very different atmospheres with them. You can almost feel the warmth of the sun or the coolness of the shady leaves from the variety of greens he uses.

They are odd-looking mountains.

The artist has mixed reality with his imagination in this painting. Of course he knew what real rocks looked like. But perhaps at home he had a collection of small pebbles whose shapes he liked. He painted them here on a grand scale, and they became huge, extraordinary-shaped mountains.

Does this landscape actually exist somewhere?

This is a fantasy landscape. You could look all over the world and never find the same scene. Some of the elements in this landscape are borrowed from reality, however. Patenier was born in the Meuse region of France, famous for its cliffs and caves, and later he moved to the south of France to a place called Baux-de-Provence. The natural scenery he saw in these places inspired him. He borrowed a shape here, a detail there—trees, houses, bushes, coastlines, a particular cloud, a little shelter—and brought them all together in this painting.

On one side of the painting everything is pointy and on the other everything is flat.

The composition of the painting illustrates different aspects of life. On the left the shapes are complicated and tall. There is a tall church and some houses at the summit of the mountain; to get to the monastery, where St. Jerome lived, required a hard and tiring climb. On the right-hand side of the picture, everything is peaceful, and the countryside is much gentler. This contrast was a way of illustrating the idea that sometimes life is hard and we have to struggle, but that, at other times, everything goes well and life seems simple.

St. Jerome is tiny in this picture; does that mean he's not important?

St. Jerome is actually very important to the meaning of the painting. He appears in the foreground, which means you must take him in before you can make sense of the rest of the painting. The landscape can be read as symbolic of his thoughts: sometimes his meditation is as peaceful as the valleys, and at other times his mental turmoil stops him in his tracks. It's as if he is on a winding road full of obstacles, and his destination is hidden from view. Moving through this painting is like entering his mind.

Is St. Jerome always painted in a landscape?

The countryside is one of two traditional settings for pictures of St. Jerome. In other paintings he is shown working in his study, writing, reading, or thinking. He was both an intellectual (he translated the Bible into Latin from the original Greek and Hebrew) and a monk (he lived as a hermit isolated from society and devoting himself to prayer). These complementary aspects of the ideal Christian life inspired painters to show him in various different settings.

There is a small cross close to St. Jerome.

Even if you don't know St. Jerome's story you can tell from that crucifix that he is a devout Christian. The way it leans against the rock opposite him almost suggests that he is in conversation with Jesus. A skull also appears next to the rock. Skulls are often featured in religious paintings to evoke the idea of the death of the first man, Adam. Together the skull and the crucifix symbolize death and redemption.

Where did the real St. Jerome live?

He lived mainly in Rome and in the Middle East. He spent five years in the desert in Syria, then lived in Bethlehem in Palestine, where he founded a monastery. He died in 420 C.E. As you can see, this landscape bears no resemblance at all to those places. Patenier never visited the Middle East and probably didn't know much about a desert landscape. Nevertheless, the green scenery here still suggests that St. Jerome is far away from the bustle of city life.

Why did the artist make the landscape more important than the person?

Patenier lived in an era of great discoveries. Thanks to the expeditions of Columbus and Vasco de Gama, among others, Europeans were finally learning about far-off lands full of untold riches. The conquistadors set off to the Americas in search of gold and the influence of Western Europe spread ever further across the globe. The wide-open spaces in Patenier's landscape reflect that new way of seeing the world. For him, painting became a way to travel and explore.

It seems like it would take a long time to cross this landscape.

Extreme distance is one of the important ideas in this painting. Appreciating the space in the landscape gives you a sense of time passing. There are no direct routes but plenty of diversions and obstacles. The painting suggests multiple pathways. It is easy to imagine yourself within the landscape choosing a direction and heading into the unknown. Even at its very farthest point the picture opens up new possibilities: all you would have to do is board one of the ships at the coast. Patenier lived in Antwerp, one of the largest ports in Europe, and these ships must have been a familiar sight.

As you get toward the horizon the land turns turquoise.

Turquoise, as a color, is rarely found in nature but it often appears in Patenier's work. It's a mixture of green and blue and, in this way, belongs as much to plants as it does to the sky. The green of the fields becomes light and blue like the sky and the blue of the sky takes on the color of the fields. It's as though nature has changed its mind, and the colors you take for granted have been transformed. There is something almost magical about a turquoise landscape.

Is this a religious painting or a landscape?

It's both a religious painting and a landscape. The saint gives the image a religious foundation, and the landscape can be interpreted as a metaphor for the Christian journey toward salvation. But St. Jerome's life also provides a perfect pretext for painting a landscape: instead of the scenery being simply a backdrop, here it evokes the idea of limitless space. Patenier invented a new kind of painting, one rooted in the tradition of religious subjects that also gives prominence to the landscape. In a sense, it is with him that landscape painting was truly born.

8 Portrait of Charles V at Mühlberg

Painted about 1548; oil on canvas; 332 x 279 cm
The Prado Museum, Madrid, Spain
Titian (Tiziano Vecellio, known as Titian, Pieve di Cadore)
Born 1488/1489; died in Venice 1576

Where was this painting meant to be hung?

This painting was designed to be hung in a palace with very large, high walls. Its large size meant that it could be seen easily. If it had been smaller, it would have made less impact and might have been overlooked among the other paintings.

Who is the knight?

This is no ordinary knight. This is Charles V, an emperor who ruled over several countries at once (Spain, the Netherlands, Germany, Austria, and parts of what are now France and Italy) during the early sixteenth century.

Is he a warrior?

Yes; he had just won a very important battle, and, to mark the occasion, he asked his favorite artist, Titian, to come and paint his portrait. His armor is of the finest quality, he is carrying a lance, and his horse is protected by a red caparison (a sort of cape). He wanted everyone who saw the painting to know that he was a great soldier.

Where is his army?

The army can't be far away, but Charles didn't want other soldiers in the picture. Nor did he want to show the battle itself. The painting conveys his powerfulness without showing exactly what happened on the battlefield.

It looks like he's coming out of a forest.

Forests can be terrifying places: they are dark and, in that era, they were still home to wild animals and bandits. By showing the trees behind Charles V, Titian shows how exceptionally brave he is, capable of traveling calmly through a place where others wouldn't dare set foot.

♦ ♦ ♦

It looks as if the battle hasn't started yet.

The horse is stamping; he's impatient to start galloping, but the emperor is reining him in. He'll let the horse spring forward in a moment. The painting shows the emperor's wisdom—he is able to take his time and avoid rushing while still keeping up his guard. He is ready to go into battle as soon as the moment is right.

Who is he aiming at with his lance?

He has no need to aim it at anyone specifically at this moment. You can tell he is capable of facing any danger and any enemy no matter who or what they might be. But, before the attack, he is sitting upright and looks totally calm. The lance's position in his hand symbolizes the warrior's desire for battle.

There are many clouds in the sky.

The artist has added life to his painting with a sky full of movement and color. The horizon is still bright, but the day will soon be ending. This is another way of showing the emperor's power: he is full of vigor and energy even at the end of the day. He will keep watch until the last minute.

The horse wouldn't have been able to hold that pose while the painter was working.

Usually, in paintings that featured horses, the subject would pose on an artificial horse so the artist could capture the general position, and the details were filled in later. The emperor did not have the time to pose for too long or too often, but the artist tried to make sure that the end result was as lifelike as possible.

Was the painting done outside?

Painting outside would not have been practical, especially at a time of war. Like most artists at the time, Titian worked in a studio. He painted the people and the landscapes separately but would meld them together seamlessly. However, there's no way of knowing if the scenery in this painting is anything like the location where the battle really took place.

Why did Titian paint the emperor on his horse?

His aim was to create a painting that would convey Charles V's power. He needed to do something spectacular. So he adapted a convention from ancient sculpture: the equestrian statue. He was especially inspired by a statue of the Roman emperor Marcus Aurelius, and he modified the pose to put the focus on action. Although Titian's portrait commemorates a particular moment in Charles V's life it also underlines the qualities the two emperors shared: courage, greatness, and wisdom.

Are there many equestrian portraits?

Many kings and emperors copied Charles V and had themselves painted mounted on their horses. An equestrian portrait became an essential symbol of power. Following in Titian's footsteps, other artists introduced variations in both the pose of the horse and the look of the rider. Different works highlight different aspects of the model—his nobility, his elegance, or his enthusiasm. Eventually wealthy people who were neither kings nor emperors began to have themselves painted in this way. It was less costly than a statue.

The horse isn't all that big.

If Titian had painted the horse in proper proportion, it would have taken up more of the picture than the rider, and the emperor's greatness would have been diminished. The viewer should not notice the horse before the man. So, the artist altered reality. But he managed to do it so subtly that people rarely notice it when they first see the painting.

Is that how the armor and the lance actually looked?

This is an exact representation of the armor worn by Charles V at his victory at Mühlberg. It was a unique, richly worked suit of armor, and it was important for it to be recognizable and admired in the painting. But the most important feature was the lance. According to legend it was the "Holy Lance" used to pierce Christ's side when he was on the cross. Forty-five emperors had owned this relic before Charles. It was even said that Charlemagne kept it by his side at all times, even when he was asleep, as if it was a talisman.

When you look at the painting close up, the emperor doesn't seem quite so impressive.

Behind any royal title, there is always a human being who is as fragile as any other. The artist has used very subtle light and coloring, and his brushstrokes are so small that the portrait seems very lifelike. Such almost imperceptible details make Charles appear more human and vulnerable. You can imagine him thinking and feeling. Looking at the portrait close up gives us an intimate impression of the subject as well as enabling us to see the skill with which it was painted.

Did Titian know Charles V well?

Titian had painted him several times before and had had the opportunity to observe him closely, which helped the artist understand what he expected from his portraits. Titian captured the authority of his subjects as well as their humanity, sensitivity, and strength—an invaluable gift for a court painter. Charles V knew that Titian would show him in all his glory without neglecting his gravitas and thoughtfulness. At the time of a great victory over the Protestants, he was the greatest of the Catholic rulers. The portrait he had commissioned had to celebrate his power, but he also wanted it to show his longing for peace. Away from the realities of the battlefield he thought this battle should be understood, above all, as a spiritual one.

9 Winter Landscape with a Bird Trap

Painted 1565; oil on wood; 38 x 56 cm
The Brussels Museum, Brussels, Belgium
(Musées royaux des Beaux Arts, Brussels)
Pieter Bruegel the Elder
Born about 1525/1530; died in Brussels 1569

This painting looks Christmassy.

It's not particularly a Christmas scene, but it shows winter as we like to imagine it, with plenty of snow. The houses at each side and in the background give us the impression of being sheltered by the village. Sometimes it's fun to feel cold when you know you can go inside and warm up.

It may be very cold, but it's very sunny.

The whole painting is bathed in a golden light the color of honey. When you see it from a distance, it's probably the first thing you notice. That lovely color is a big part of the reason why the picture is so appealing. Even if you just catch a glimpse of it in passing, it is pleasing.

What are the people doing?

The people in the painting are skating on the frozen river. In the mid-sixteenth century, they didn't have the sophisticated skates we have now: they just attached wooden blades to their shoes. It looks like it worked pretty well.

The people look like little ants.

Though the painting is small, Breugel can include the whole scene because he is painting it from a distance. You can see people appear tiny and black, sliding in every direction, scuttling like insects or like birds hopping about in the snow.

There are also some big black birds.

They're crows. They're perched in the branches and seem a lot more peaceful than the other birds. It looks as if they are waiting for something, watching what's happening. People can be a bit like that too: some are always busy and others are more patient.

♦ ♦ ♦

The people are all doing something different.

All the characters in the painting are different ages, and everyone has his or her own character and is doing something different. When you look at them individually, you can see that some are chatting while others are hurrying on their way. One is balancing on one leg, and there's a mother holding her child by the hand, walking more slowly. Some are in pairs and others are alone. Some of the skaters aren't that steady on their feet.

No one has fallen over.

These people must be used to skating. This is an ordinary, everyday scene from their lives. In the painting it looks as though everyone is in control, but there could still be an accident. At any moment someone could easily fall over. Some are being very careful, and others are probably just lucky.

What if the ice broke?

We can't tell how thick the ice is, and it could give way under the weight of a skater. At the bottom of the painting there's already a hole. Even though people are taking care, there is always a chance that something dangerous could happen. Some things are simply beyond their control. You can imagine the painter thinking about these things as he watched the people enjoying themselves.

What are the wooden planks on the right of the picture?

It's a bird trap, which would be a common sight for these country folk. A threat even hangs over the birds; neither people nor animals are ever completely safe.

The perspective of the painting is as if we're looking down from high on a hill.

The vantage point is certainly higher than the river and is some distance away. On the one hand you might feel safe there—the skaters are far enough away that there is no danger of colliding with one of them and falling over. But on the other hand, the bushes and trees in the foreground don't look very safe for leaning on—dead branches break easily. Perhaps this vantage point is no safer than the ice after all.

You can see the village church.

As the religious center of the village, the church has an important role. By including it in the painting, Breugel evokes another dimension in the lives of these people he has painted enjoying themselves. In the picture they are scattered about, each going about his or her different business, but from time to time they gather together at the church. The church conveys the idea of unity between the people and perhaps of refuge.

Did Breugel live in this village?

Breugel first worked at Antwerp, and in 1565 when he painted this picture, he was living in Brussels. But this village isn't far from Brussels; it's in the same region, Brabant. Breugel painted it so faithfully that historians think it is possible to identify which village it really was: they believe it is a place called Pede-Sainte-Anne. The area appears in so many of his paintings that it is now known as Breugel valley.

The artist has used very few colors.

It's very difficult to paint an image with so few colors, but it makes it exciting because very minor variations in shade can bring tiny details to life. Breugel has used few colors, and the painting feels homogenous. He makes the most of the limited palette: white, a little black, and many shades of brown, ochre, and yellow (particularly toward the horizon).

Why is Breugel called "the Elder"? Was he very old?

That's often what people think, especially because he is sometimes also known as Old Breugel. In fact Breugel the Elder had a very short life. He was only about forty when he died. But this nickname is to distinguish him from his sons, who were also painters. His eldest son, Breugel the Younger, was also called Pieter. His second son, Jan, used such soft colors that he became known as "Velvet Breugel."

The crows are a bit menacing.

Crows are often believed to have unpleasant connotations because they are black. It is possible that in this painting they represent death. But the same object can often symbolize many different ideas, depending on the context and who is looking at it. In ancient Rome, for example, people viewed crows as a symbol of hope because the noise they make, "cra cra," sounds like the Latin word for tomorrow, *cras*.

Is there a lesson behind this painting?

It certainly seems to be about people being dwarfed by nature and living under the shadow of all sorts of potential threats. But Breugel isn't mocking his subjects or criticizing them. He simply observes things as they are. Just as his landscape captures both the winter cold and the warmth of the sun, there is a balance in the world between danger and fun.

10 David with the Head of Goliath

Painted about 1606; oil on wood; 90.5 x 116 cm
Kunsthistorisches Museum, Vienna, Austria
Caravaggio (Michelangelo Merisi, known as Caravaggio)
Born Caravaggio 1571; died Port-Ercole, 1610

The boy is holding a head by the hair.

He's the David from the Bible story. He is holding up the head of the giant Goliath, whom he has just killed.

Why did he kill him?

The Bible says that David defended his people against their enemies, who were led by Goliath. By killing their leader he defeated the whole army.

Did he cut Goliath's head off?

Yes, but he killed him first. He threw a stone at Goliath with his sling and killed him with the first hit. Then he took the giant's sword and cut off his head with it to prove that Goliath was finally defeated.

Goliath doesn't have a very big head for a giant.

That's true, but if the artist had painted the head any larger he wouldn't have had enough room to show David, who is, after all, the hero of the story. That's why Goliath's head is more or less normal size.

David isn't dressed like a soldier.

He was a simple shepherd and refused the armor that King Saul offered him, preferring to fight in his tunic. His only weapon was a sling and five stones. The giant had a coat of chain mail, a helmet, a javelin, and a sword. The painter depicted the end of the story to highlight David's courage.

What does he have in his bag?

He probably has the rest of the stones he'd collected, even though he only needed one to kill Goliath. It looks like the bag contains everything he owns—not much. He's holding a sword, which he's just taken from the giant.

How did humble David manage to beat a giant?

Goliath was obviously bigger and stronger, but his size was his downfall: it made him an easy target for the shepherd, who was a good shot with his sling. Goliath wasn't afraid of such a small, weak boy. But David had agility and intelligence on his side. Goliath's size, which had been his strength, became his vulnerable point, and David's weakness became his opportunity.

Was Goliath really all that big?

The term "giant" was just a way to express his exceptional strength and size. When people come across an obstacle so large that they don't know how to get around it, it appears gigantic. No doubt the people who were facing Goliath saw him like that, and David certainly did when he faced him alone.

What happens next?

After defeating Goliath, David had to flee from King Saul, who was jealous of his success. But such a hero, capable of defeating a giant, deserved to lead his people and that is how a humble shepherd boy became the king of Israel. David was a brave soldier, a poet, and a musician, and he had an equally famous son, King Solomon (14). These tales are told in the Old Testament.

David doesn't look very pleased to have defeated Goliath.

He looks serious rather than triumphant. No doubt he is glad to have done his duty, but Caravaggio doesn't show him happy about killing Goliath. The giant's death is treated with respect: Goliath's face shows his suffering. The victory is not about personal satisfaction; it's for all of his people, the Israelites.

Why is there no one other than David in the painting?

When the fight took place, it's likely that there was a huge crowd of people—countless soldiers waiting to see who would win the battle. But at the key moment, David must have felt very alone, with everything depending on him. He wanted to concentrate without being distracted by the people around him. Caravaggio has chosen to convey that sense of solitude.

Why is the painting so dark?

The black background makes the characters stand out. Caravaggio often used this technique—ignoring scenery, landscapes, and props, focusing on just a few key elements. In this way he makes his scenes easier to understand as well as more dramatic. His paintings would have been seen by candle- or lamplight in the era when they were painted, unlike the way his paintings are lit in galleries today. Seen like that, the figures in his paintings must really have looked ghostly.

Goliath's head looks as though it is coming out of the painting.

David is holding it out toward us, and the almost three-dimensional effect is strengthened by the contrast between the black background and the well-lit shapes. Caravaggio's sense of lighting works like a projector. The brightly lit parts of the painting seem to jump forward as if they were in relief. This technique makes the scene fascinating: we feel as though we could reach out and touch the characters.

Did Caravaggio always paint people in relief?

In most of his paintings he focuses more on the relief effect than on the depth of the composition. In a sense, it's impossible to "enter" his paintings—the background is empty, just a black wall. On the other hand, the characters almost seem to leap out of the painting. Rather than being a spectator passively standing in front of a painting, the viewer feels like a witness to an unexpected scene. The surprise is immense.

Why did the painter choose this precise moment in the story of David and Goliath?

The presentation of the *fait accompli* creates a shocking effect. This is obviously the conclusion of the battle. Even if you don't know the story of David and Goliath from the Bible, their presence in the painting is immediately arresting. The image is frozen in space and time: in space because there is no background, and in time because the scene itself is as swift as a blink of the eye.

Was a painting like this intended to be hung in a church?

No, it was not intended for a place of worship. This type of painting was for sophisticated art lovers, who were beginning to establish vast collections in that era. These connoisseurs would have the education necessary to understand the depth of meaning in a painting like this. It was not designed to support the worship of the faithful; it was meant to appeal to the intellect of the collectors.

Did other painters do this kind of painting?

Caravaggio invented this kind of painting based on the sharp distinction between light and dark. He lived in Rome and, during his lifetime at the beginning of the seventeenth century, artists were flocking to that city from all over Europe to study their art, visit the ancient monuments, and see the important works of the Renaissance. Caravaggio's work was enormously successful at that time, and even today his work still has the immediacy of a live television broadcast or the spectacle of a grand opera. Many Italian, French, Dutch, and Spanish painters followed his example, and now the term Caravaggism is used to describe that style.

11 The Cardsharp with the Ace of Clubs

Painted about 1625–30; oil on canvas mounted on wood; 96.5 x 155 cm
Kimbell Art Museum, Fort Worth, United States of America
Georges de La Tour
Born at Vic-sur-Seilles in the bishopric of Metz 1593; died Luneville 1652

They're playing cards.
The three people sitting down are in the middle of a game of cards, but there is one person who isn't playing: the woman standing up holding a bottle. She's a servant.

One of them is cheating!
The man on the left is hiding cards in his belt. They catch your eye immediately because they are white, and he looks like he wants you to notice them. In fact, the artist shows you he's cheating to explain the story.

Can't the others see they are playing with a cheat?
The man opposite the cheat, or cardsharp, has no idea and is busy studying his cards. Yes, it's good that he's thinking carefully before taking his turn, but he also doesn't realize what kind of person he's playing with.

The people are very well dressed.
Yes they are, especially the young man on the right. His clothes shine (they're probably made of very expensive fabric embroidered with silver), and his hat is decorated with a large feather. Everyone can see that he is rich, but he is unguarded and likely to attract thieves. The seated woman, wearing an elegant dress and pearl necklace, also looks wealthy. By contrast the cardsharp isn't wearing anything eye-catching because he doesn't want to draw attention to himself.

Are the women in cahoots with the cheat?
They probably are. The three of them form a group in the picture—their hands are very close together and the ladies are whispering. The woman in the red hat is turned slightly toward her two accomplices and is talking to them, but the young man seems distracted, cut off in his own little world, his gold pieces in front of him.

The two women look funny because they are both looking out of the corner of their eyes.
They don't want to draw attention to their scheming. If the woman in the red hat turned her head completely to the side, the young man beside them might notice and become suspicious. However, right now, he is quite oblivious. The servant looks as though she is quickly glancing at the cardsharp.

Why is there only one glass of wine?
It's probably for the rich young man. The others have to keep a clear head if they want to get away with their trickery. If he is a little bit drunk he'll be less aware of the trouble he's in. And the maid will have a chance to look at his cards when she puts the glass down on the table in front of him.

You can't tell where this is taking place.
The painter doesn't show the setting; maybe it's a tavern. But a scene like this could take place almost anywhere. The world is full of cheats and tricksters. This painting shows a general truth rather than a specific story.

The woman's head looks like an egg.
Georges de La Tour liked to paint very simple, almost geometric shapes. This woman has a very smooth face, and nothing moves except her eyes. She is controlling herself very well. Though she is well lit and we see her features clearly, all we really see is her surface appearance. It's impossible to guess what she is thinking.

No one is speaking.
They are all waiting to see how the game will turn out. Nothing has happened yet, but we sense that the moment of truth will soon come. The cardsharp is getting ready to take out the card he has hidden in his belt. Soon all the gold pieces will be changing hands.

Why is there light behind only one of the characters?
The placing of light and shade emphasizes the relationships between the figures. The only area that is lit is a small piece of wall behind the young man who is being duped. The other three appear against a black background, showing that they belong together. The fact that the black area is so much larger than the lighted area shows that the tricksters are stronger than their opponent. The respective areas of innocence and trickery are clearly defined.

Why is the cardsharp's face not as well lit as the other faces?
He turns his back to the light because he is deceitful by nature. Even if the young man were to look at him, he wouldn't see much. With his back to the light, his face is in shadow. This position gives him the advantage over the young man because he can see perfectly well without being seen himself.

Has the young man got a chance?
To avoid trouble, he just has to lift his eyes. If he did so, he might notice that the other players are in league against him. He needs to pay attention to what is going on around him, but at the moment he can't see farther than the end of his nose. He doesn't suspect a thing and his *naïveté* will be his downfall. The others are malicious, and he needs to realize that they know how to get what they want. He is still very young; they appear more worldly and wise.

What game are they playing?

Anyone who saw the painting in the seventeenth century would automatically have recognized that the game is Prime. To win, a player had to collect the highest number of points in the same color, the maximum score being fifty-five. The cardsharp has at least a six (eighteen points) or a seven (twenty-one points) in his hand. With the ace, which is worth sixteen points, he is very likely to win the hand.

The cardsharp has clubs and the young man has spades.

Cards have a symbolic language of their own. Though it wasn't part of the rules of the game, the artist may have dictated these distinctions as a commentary or to give the picture extra significance. Clubs signify money. Spades in the victim's hand herald nothing but problems. La Tour actually painted another painting with exactly the same subject and composition. It was identical except for a few details and colors. But the cheat in that picture is holding an ace of diamonds, which suggests a fruitful outcome.

Why are the characters so squashed up in the painting?

By giving the characters very little space the artist creates a heavy atmosphere. It feels like there isn't much air and it's hard to breathe. The tightly framed scene also accentuates how closely the characters are linked. As a result you become aware of everything. You can notice even the slightest bat of an eyelid, and every detail takes on significance.

Why did Georges de La Tour paint such an unfair story?

The painting shows that if you want to avoid the same sort of dangerous situation you have to be more careful and alert than this young man. It's putting across a moral lesson. Young men risk losing everything unless they are on their guard against women who want to seduce them, and unless they avoid getting drunk and never gamble. In the seventeenth century those were the three most feared dangers. The painting combines them to make the warning even more effective.

12 Apollo and Marsyas

Painted 1637; oil on canvas; 182 x 232 cm
Museo Nazionale di San Martino, Naples, Italy
Jusepe de Ribera
Born at Jativa, Valence province, 1591; died Naples 1652

Who are these people?
The one at the top is Apollo, the sun god. The other is named Marsyas; he is a satyr and has the body of a man and the legs of a deer. They are both characters from Greek mythology.

What are they doing?
Apollo is punishing Marsyas by ripping off his skin. The punishment has just started. Marsyas is crying out in pain.

Why is Marsyas being punished?
Marsyas was so proud of how well he played the flute that he challenged Apollo to a contest. Apollo played the viol or the lyre and Marsyas played the flute. Apollo won. It had been agreed that the winner would punish the loser in whatever way he saw fit, so Apollo decided to skin him alive.

Apollo doesn't look angry.
His calm expression shows that he's not doing it because he is angry. He's not doing it for pleasure or because he is mean. He is a god, and it would be beneath him to be affected by the scene.

Apollo's body is very white.
He is the god of the sun. Each morning he makes the day break, and then crosses the sky in his chariot. He is always shown as a radiant character with golden hair and a peaceful face.

Marsyas has dark skin.
The contrast with Apollo had to be clear: unlike the sun god he is not radiant. He lives in the shadows of the forest and has taken on the color of the trees. His skin is rough. He is half man and half beast, and his thighs are covered in dark fur.

The painting is divided in two; one half is bright and the other dark.

Even without looking at the details you can tell immediately that the painting shows two different and opposing worlds: the world of the sky and light, where the god Apollo belongs, and the world of the earth and darkness, where the satyr Marsyas belongs. They cannot mix or merge. Marsyas is punished because he dared to think he could equal the gods.

Why does Apollo have leaves on his head?

He is wearing the crown of laurels. In ancient times athletes who won the games held in stadiums were given crowns like this. Laurel leaves stay green all year round, and so they symbolize immortality, one of Apollo's godly attributes.

There's a musical instrument on the ground.

That's a viol, an ancient sort of violin. It belongs to Apollo. He put it down on the ground after the contest so that he could punish Marsyas. Its position in the foreground is a reminder of the beginning of this gruesome story. Stringed instruments were thought to have a much gentler, clearer, and nobler sound than wind instruments such as Marsyas's flute.

Who are the people behind the tree?

They are satyrs, friends of Marsyas. Like him, they are the wood- and mountain-dwelling spirit companions of the god Bacchus. They are horrified, watching their friend being tortured, unable to do anything to help him. One of them covers his ears so that he can't hear Marsyas's screams. According to the legend they cried so much that they created a river of tears. Ribera painted these figures in grey colors to show that they were simply spectators. But their presence is necessary. What happens to Marsyas serves as a lesson: they have now been warned of the dangers of comparing oneself to a god.

Why is Marsyas's face darker than his body?

The artist used real models to paint their bodies accurately. The face of the person who posed as Marsyas might have been much more tanned than his body, and Ribera didn't change that. It makes the character seem more lifelike. By contrast, Apollo's coloring is uniform because he symbolizes light. Unlike Marsyas, the god's body does not have the same weaknesses that a human body does.

You can see brushstrokes in the sky.

The top of the picture is painted much more lightly than the rest of it, with subtle, iridescent, shimmering colors, whereas at the bottom opaque browns and black predominate. Apollo's pink cloak links the two sections; its folds blend gently with the shapes of the clouds. Apollo is not starkly outlined against the sky. This effect suggests the infinity of space over which the god reigns, and reminds us of the high winds that accompany him across the sky and the speed of his journey.

It looks like the two figures were painted in a circle.

At the bottom of the painting Marsyas's arms form the curve of a circle that is completed at the top by Apollo's pink cloak. You can almost imagine a circular line enclosing them. This focuses attention on the drama unfolding between them: they are in a closed world, and Marsyas will never escape from it. The circle also suggests the idea of a constantly turning wheel, a wheel that symbolizes the cycle of life and death and of night and day. Every morning, no matter what happens, Apollo reappears with the sun and banishes the darkness.

The two figures are opposites of each other.

The surface characteristics are opposite, yes—divine and animal, light and dark, and so on. But this story also illustrates the two poles of human nature: on the one hand, there is the desire to elevate oneself, and on the other, there is self-abasement. It's a fascinating subject for the artist and offers the chance to paint two complementary nudes: one suggests physical perfection and the other physical suffering.

Why did Apollo decide to skin Marsyas?

The punishment in this myth has a symbolic meaning. Skinning Marsyas means robbing him of his appearance, his mask. In other words, he who had claimed he was equal to a god would be laid bare and his true nature exposed. In symbolic terms the painting shows a fitting way to punish excessive pride.

Marsyas's punishment seems too harsh.

Yes, the punishment seems disproportionate when you think that all he did was claim he could play music as well as Apollo. That kind of boast doesn't seem so bad in and of itself. But it represents much more than that. No matter how good a musician he may have been, he's still just a player. His real crime was to have believed that his talent made him equal to a god. By punishing him so terribly, Apollo, the creator and protector of the arts, makes a distinction between skill and divine inspiration.

13 Still Life with Fruit and a Lobster

Painted 1646–49; oil on canvas; 95 x 120 cm
Gemaldegalerie, Berlin, Germany
Jan Davidsz de Heem
Born in Utrecht 1606; died Antwerp 1684

There are lots of things to eat on the table.

This kind of picture makes you hungry. It shows all sorts of fruits—grapes, peaches, apricots, and quinces—on a large, round, blue and white porcelain plate. There is also a half-peeled lemon on a smaller plate. There are prawns on the right, but perhaps the first thing you'll notice is the red lobster on the edge of the table.

The lobster might nip our fingers.

Because it's red, you know that the lobster has already been cooked, so there's no danger. If it was still alive, it would be a brownish color. But the bright red color does make him stand out; he gives the impression of being quite threatening.

Everything is jumbled up.

The fruit is piled up in no particular order. There are also some shells carefully placed on a box covered in blue velvet. In real life you probably wouldn't find these things all together, but in the picture they produce a good, vibrant mixture of colors. The effect is a bit like fireworks.

It's hard to tell what the objects are sitting on.

They're on a table. You can see this more clearly on the right-hand side of the picture. The table is almost completely covered with a dark green tablecloth, except on that part. On the left you can also see some slightly shiny folds in the fabric.

There's also something to drink.

There are three glasses in this painting. Their different shapes indicate that they contain different types of wine. The one on the right, for example, contains white wine from Alsace. The artist has given us several choices. There's something for every taste.

The pitcher is very beautiful.

This jug is called a ewer, and it's used to serve wine. This one was made from a shell with a gold setting. The light reflects off the mother-of-pearl like a mini rainbow. This kind of object wasn't used at everyday meals. The painter has highlighted it by placing it at the edge of the table and at a slight distance from the other objects.

It looks like the lobster is about to move.

That's because the color red gives an impression of liveliness, and its pinchers are dangling off the plate, as if it's trying to reach something outside the picture. The artist wanted the lobster to grab our attention, like a road sign warning of danger. Because it moves sideways, like the crab, lobsters symbolize hypocrisy. In this picture it reminds us that people get things wrong and make mistakes, and you should never be fooled by appearances.

Why isn't the lemon completely peeled?

The lemon forms a sort of visual anchor for the left-hand side of the painting. It also gives the artist an opportunity to paint a beautifully curved spiral. The half-peeled lemon is actually a common motif in still lifes. It allows de Heem to capture a stolen moment, which only lasts the span of a second. The peel is still holding on, but any moment it will fall, completely detached, from the fruit. This half-peeled lemon is a lovely way to suggest the notion of time.

Why are there shells on the table?

The shells can be admired for their refined colors and interesting shapes, but they also seem to come from far away, to contain the infinity of the ocean. Here, along with the lobster and the prawns, the shells evoke the mysteries of the seas, while the fruits and the vine leaves are reminders of land and trees.

What is the curtain for?

The curtain sets the scene, throwing the background into relief and capturing some light. It also shows that the image is not just a reproduction of an everyday table. The scene is not set in a particular room in a specific house. This is theater. The artist has invented a setting to meet the needs of his composition.

What is in the blue box?

It seems to be a jewelry box, and it probably contains some precious things that we can't see. The treasures remain hidden. The painting presents an array of objects but keeps some undisclosed. That's one of the functions of the box in this picture; it re-establishes balance by refusing to divulge its secret and reminding us that we cannot see or know everything.

Does the painting show the ingredients for a real meal?

The table setting here does not compose a menu, it creates an image of opulence. There is a mix of fruits from different seasons—such as the cherries and the grapes—and when this was painted in the middle of the seventeenth century these foods were very expensive and only available to rich people. This painting doesn't necessarily show what even the wealthiest people had on their plates every day, but it gives an idea of the kind of luxuries they could afford. The same is true of the dishes, the plates, and the carafe, which are all luxury items as well.

Why doesn't the tablecloth completely cover the table?

The fact that the cloth is slightly too small leaves the table exposed in all its unadorned simplicity. The painting is illustrating that there is a distinction between how things appear and their true nature. The cloth, both hiding and revealing the table simultaneously, plays a similar role to that of the lemon peel, which both covers and uncovers the fruit: it disguises or reveals reality.

Why is everything placed so that it could fall?

That precariousness is one of the charms of the painting. It gives both the idea of abundance and the suggestion that everything could collapse as easily as a house of cards. Things are toppling, leaning, sliding. That's the lesson behind the picture. It celebrates plenty and success but reminds you that at any moment everything could come tumbling down, in both a real and a figurative sense.

Why did the artist show a plum half eaten by worms?

The plum, in the middle of the platter next to the cherries, is a sign of how quickly things change: no one has had a chance to eat it before it became infested with worms. Other elements of the painting make the same point: the lemon is almost peeled; the wine is already poured; the lobster is cooked and ready to be eaten; the creatures that lived in the beautiful pearly shells are already dead. There's no time to lose in this life.

Were there a lot of still lifes like this?

Yes, there were and they were very successful. Jan Davidsz de Heem was one of a number of artists who specialized in this kind of painting. These artists were especially good at showing different materials and textures. They could, for example, accurately reproduce the velvety softness of a peach, the misty bloom of a grape, the cracking of a shell, or the transparency of glass. This style of painting demonstrates genuine artistic expertise and knowledge. At the same time, these still lifes struck a chord with the seventeenth-century Dutch public by showing both the richness of material things and their transience, which served as a reminder of the vanity of taking too much pleasure in them.

14 The Judgment of Solomon

Painted 1649; oil on canvas; 101 x 150 cm
The Louvre Museum, Paris, France
Nicolas Poussin
Born in Les Andelys 1594; died in Rome 1665

What is this painting about?

It tells the story of two women who came to see King Solomon, who was known for his wisdom. The women lived in the same house and each had a baby. One night one of the babies died, and each woman claimed that the survivor was hers.

Is it a true story?

King Solomon did exist, a long time ago. He was the son of King David, who killed the giant Goliath (10). His story is told in the Bible and this episode is an example of what a just ruler he was.

Where is King Solomon?

The king is seated on his throne, pronouncing his judgment, high above the other characters and their squabbles. He is at the center of the picture because everyone is waiting for his decision. If he were leaning to one side or the other, or if he were anything other than absolutely in the middle, you would get the impression that he was favoring one woman over the other. He holds himself upright, and this shows that he is absolutely just and fair.

There are people on both sides.

These people are spectators watching the scene. Like us they are wondering what's going to happen. Some of them look worried. One of them looks serious; perhaps he already has an idea of how things will turn out. Others are so alarmed that they have to look away.

It looks as though the soldier on the left is about to kill the baby.

Both women are claiming that this living baby is theirs. So King Solomon has ordered the soldier to cut it in two and let each woman have half. Of course he has no intention of having the baby killed; it is just a trick to get a reaction from the women. One of them must be lying about being the mother, and the king has devised this trap to find out which one it is.

What's going to happen?

The woman in yellow is begging the king to spare the child, and she declares that it is not hers. She loves the baby so much that she would rather give it up than see it killed. This is how Solomon knows that she is the true mother. By simply lifting a finger he gives the order for the baby to be returned to her.

♦ ♦ ♦

How can we tell what the women are saying?

You can tell what they're saying just by observing their body language. The woman on the right looks neither at the king nor at the baby; she is neither sad nor considering what is just. She is simply there to accuse the other woman. She is pointing at her, green with envy. She doesn't even care if the child is chopped in half or not. The woman in yellow, however, is not looking for a fight. She is turned toward the king, begging him for mercy, thinking only of the child.

Why do the people's gestures seem so unnatural?
The poses are exaggerated because each movement is translating a feeling or a state of mind. The story and the motivations of the protagonists have to be clear immediately. Their whole bodies are used to express their emotions. It's like a ballet or mime.

Did the artist use living models?
The artist, Poussin, painted this picture after a long period of preparation. During that time he did study live models, but he also was inspired by Greek and Roman statues. He used the statues to create his characters' poses and the live models for their proportions and shapes. As was customary in the seventeenth century, he made numerous drawings before he started to paint.

Do the colors have any meaning?
The colors would help tell the story even if a viewer didn't know all the details. You would be able to tell that the character in red, Solomon, is the most important because his color dominates all the others. The woman on the left is dressed in light colors—the colors of the sky and the sun—because her conscience is clear. The other woman, the liar, is darker, and her coloring is autumnal.

It's hard to tell where it all takes place.
Poussin hasn't put any emphasis on the palace itself. The throne and the two columns are enough to suggest the king's power and grandeur. As a result nothing distracts the viewer's attention from the action. The impression created by the vertical lines of the architecture and the floor tiles is more important than a detailed rendering of an opulent palace. The room as it is depicted here provides a stark, simple backdrop against which the characters' grand gestures stand out clearly. Their agitation is all the more evident against the simplicity of the lines.

It's like a scene from a play.
Each character is like an actor who must stand in a particular spot for us to understand his or her role. Poussin has laid out the scene like a theatrical director—in fact, he often used to make miniature sets in which he would place wax figurines of the characters who were to appear in his picture. This model gave him a general feeling for the scene of the painting and also allowed him to observe the way the light and shadow would fall on each figure.

Why are the expressions so exaggerated?

Poussin used the masks worn by actors in classical dramas as inspiration. Their exaggerated expressions enabled the audience to see how they were feeling, even from the back of an amphitheater. These masks were not designed to look like any one person's face but symbolized characters confronted by events and situations significant to people in general. The masks also helped to amplify the actors' voices, so the characters' expressions in the painting, by suggesting the masks, actually bring a dimension of sound to the image. The characters on the sides are like a Greek chorus commenting on the action.

Every detail is filled with meaning.

Yes, everything included here counts. Poussin wanted to show that every action has inevitable consequences. He played with the fact that, in a two-dimensional painting, different elements, though perhaps far from one another in the actual scene, are squashed together on the canvas. For example, the woman in yellow opens her arms and gives up the child, but she appears to embrace the baby even though the soldier is actually holding it beyond her reach. The way the shapes coincide shows that by giving up the child she is proving her love, and as a result, the baby will be returned to her. For another example, the mother's agony is shown quite clearly: the sword that will kill the child is actually pointed toward her body. She is already suffering the fate that could face the child. The other woman appears crushed by the weight of justice because the column behind her looks as if it's resting on her neck.

How did Poussin choose the subjects for his paintings?

Poussin liked to paint subjects that gave him the chance to reflect on a problem. The collectors of the period, several of whom were his friends, appreciated his work enough to trust him to choose his own subjects. That was the case with this painting. The desire for the freedom to choose the subjects that interested him, and not his patrons, is one of the reasons why, although he was French, Poussin preferred to work in Italy. In Italy, he was far from the French court and the constraints it would have imposed on him. He had worked in France for two years and had been overwhelmed with official commissions.

Was Poussin happy with this painting?

This painting was one of his favorites. He knew that he had succeeded in conveying the profundity of a tragedy with great simplicity. He illustrated the intensity of powerful emotions—known in the seventeenth century as the "passions of the soul"—but set them against an ideal of reason that he always admired. King Solomon embodies that reason with his ability to distinguish truth from lies, rise above the crisis, and settle the case for the best. Poussin paid homage to the ancient ruler by giving him a perfectly balanced form, symbolizing absolute justice.

15 The Love Letter

Painted 1669; oil on canvas; 44 x 38 cm
Rijksmuseum, Amsterdam, Holland
Johannes Vermeer (Vermeer of Delft)
Born at Delft 1632; died at Delft 1675

This painting looks like the inside of a box.

It gives the impression that you could walk right into it, like you would walk into a house. We are in it, a little hidden in the shadows, and as we look into the next room, we see two women there.

Who are the two women?

We don't know their names. Even though the painting illustrates the scene with very specific details, it isn't about the particular individuals. The artist's aim was to make their story seem as vivid and real as possible.

What are they doing in this room?

One of the women is sitting down, holding a musical instrument. She is not playing it, however, because she is holding a letter. The other woman is standing. From their physical positions, but especially from their clothing, we understand that there is a social difference between them; one is an elegant lady and the other is a maid. The maid has just brought in the letter.

The yellow dress is very eye-catching.

The artist draws our attention to the seated woman who is receiving the letter. Someone wrote the letter, someone else collected it and brought it to this house, and here it is, finally delivered to the woman herself. The way she is lit highlights her important role in this chain of events: the light from outside shines onto her dress, making her pearls gleam.

The maid's bonnet is bright white.

The maid's bonnet, collar, and apron are the lightest points in the whole painting. She is responsible for the upkeep of the house, and the whiteness of her linen proves that she is good at her job. In the seventeenth century, Holland had the reputation of being the cleanest country in Europe. Houses were often washed from top to bottom, which created such a damp atmosphere that travelers complained that this practice made them catch cold.

There are some shoes and a broom in the doorway.

The maid must have been busy washing the floor when the letter arrived. She interrupted her work and left her things on the floor to take the letter to her mistress. Her sleeves are rolled up; it is easy to imagine her wiping her hands on her apron as she takes off her clogs.

What is in the right-hand side of the picture?

There is a chair covered in dark velvet, decorated with golden nails, with some papers and cloths left on it. The maid hasn't finished tidying up. It's a dark part of the painting, hidden a little by the artist, as if he's saying, "Come on in! Please ignore the mess!"—which of course just makes you notice the mess all the more. Vermeer is deliberately showing something perhaps we ought not to see.

What is the large curtain for?

In Vermeer's era, a thick velvet curtain would be used to stop drafts in a cold house. The painter notes aspects of daily life and plays with them in his picture. By lifting the curtain he lets in both the cold air and the viewer. In this way the painting also becomes a form of theater.

What is the black thing close to the basket?

It's a cushion where the woman would place her embroidery or sewing. Perhaps the large wicker basket contains clothes to be mended. In any case the lady of the house got bored with it and has set it aside. Maybe music suited her state of mind better than needlework at that time. The painting catches her in an intimate moment, when she was letting her mind wander, looking melancholy. That's how the maid found her when she brought in the letter.

What are the paintings on the wall?

They are landscapes. The one at the bottom is a seascape with a boat and a shining sky. The other shows a view of the countryside, with someone walking, and the weather is not so good. At that time in Holland, even if you weren't a collector, it was quite common to have paintings in your home. Paintings were part of the decor, like pieces of furniture, and Vermeer often used them in his paintings to suggest the feelings of his subjects. The paintings here tell us that the woman's thoughts are elsewhere.

What does the letter say?

That's the question! We'll never know. Nor will we ever know who wrote it. But the artist has thrown in a few clues. The recipient is dressed well and takes good care of her appearance. The paintings above her suggest her thoughts are wandering far from domestic chores. Having hurried to deliver the letter, the maid is now lingering to see the lady's reaction. Music suggests the search for harmony. All these clues lead us to guess that it is a love letter.

Why aren't the two women talking?

Nothing needs to be said. They don't have to say a name or express a feeling with words. What they have to say is communicated through looks, through the attention they are giving to each other. All Vermeer's paintings focus on such moments. His work places importance on the sudden silence that falls because a tiny change has interrupted the normal course of events. The music has stopped, the women do not speak, and the room is silent. You could stand in front of the painting forever, waiting for something to happen, for the spell to be broken.

Why are all the bright colors at the center of the painting?

The bright colors guide our eyes to the center of the painting and represent the heart of the story. The house is a refuge, solid and comfortable, but the people bring the interior thoughts and feelings. The energy begins to resonate with the two women. The yellow and the blue of their dresses are opposites—like warmth and cold, darkness and light—reminding us that life is an eternal cycle: the sun shines and night falls, the weather changes from fair to rainy. These environmental changes echo the lady's changing emotions—she burns with passion or suddenly cools.

Why did the artist use so many straight lines?

The geometric shapes give this painting a very strong structure. With the use of vertical and horizontal lines, Vermeer establishes order and balance and creates an illusion of depth. The lines on the floor lead your eyes to the women, and the lines of the door and the chimney frame them. Everything is in its place. Yet within this strict framework something irrational is happening. She may be in a rational, well-ordered world but nothing can stop this woman's heart from trembling.

16 The Colossus, or Panic

Painted 1808–10; oil on canvas; 116 x 105 cm
Prado Museum, Madrid, Spain
Francisco de Goya
Born at Fuentetodos, Aragon, 1746; died Bordeaux 1828

It's a giant!

The painting is called *The Colossus*, which is the same thing as giant. This colossus is larger than a mountain, and he must be extremely strong because his muscles are huge.

What's his name?

He doesn't have a name. No one knows who he is. He looks angry because his fists are clenched, but we don't know why or who he's angry with.

Where does he come from?

It's impossible to tell where the giant has come from. Perhaps he has come from the other side of the world, or maybe he suddenly appeared in the sky. Half his body emerges from the horizon, which means that the giant must be very far away, but because of his large size he looks very close. You can't really tell where he is.

Is he going to come back?

He seems to be walking, and though we can't tell what direction he is going to take, we can tell he's on the move. He is heavy, and his footsteps disturb the clouds and make the earth shake.

Everyone is running away.

It's hard to make out individual people because there are so many of them and they are so far away, but it's easy to tell that they are running away. There are several convoys of wagons, people on horseback, people on foot, and even herds of cattle running along on their own. They are not traveling in an organized fashion, and they are heading off in all sorts of directions.

Why isn't the little donkey moving?

Donkeys have a reputation for being very stubborn, and this one, toward the bottom of the picture, is a perfect example: everyone is hurrying away, but he is very resolutely staying put. Maybe he is so terrified that he can't move. You can imagine the screams and shouts and noise from the stream of people, yet the donkey is standing in the middle of it all, frozen.

Do the people have any hope of escaping from the colossus?

He could crush dozens of people with a single blow. But will he? The painting shows him as a threat, and perhaps the worst aspect is that no one knows what to expect. If he attacked, the people would have no hope of defending themselves.

Maybe the people are running away from something else?

It's possible that the people are afraid of something else that we can't see. After all, there is no real evidence to suggest that the colossus is acting with aggression toward them. You could even imagine that the giant, who is turning in the direction they have come from, is ready to defend them. They are heading toward us, but perhaps they are not fleeing from him—perhaps he is holding back whatever the unseen threat is.

What are the people afraid of?

They are so frightened that they have fled taking almost nothing with them, although they may not have much to take. And it's not just a few individuals but streams of people who have left their homes and become refugees. The television news shows people like these almost every day, people surrounded by catastrophes and war. These people have no choice but to do whatever they can to stay alive.

Why didn't Goya just paint a war?

He is showing an aspect of war that is not seen very often in paintings. Painters usually show battles, heroes, and victories. But Goya chose to paint a different point of view: that of average people. They aren't making war on anyone, and in many cases they don't even know what the war is about. It happens *to* them. They probably don't know much more about the situation than we, as spectators in front of the painting, do. All they know is that they have to flee, with their heads down, scattering over the land at random. The colossus is so huge that they can't even see it clearly; the threat hangs over them like a black storm cloud.

Why did Goya paint an imaginary creature?

It makes the painting more complex. The colossus can represent a war or any kind of danger that frightens people. On the other hand, he could be coming to save the people from some other enemy. Then again he might not represent anything frightening at all but fear itself, fear that overcomes us and drives us mad. That's why the painting is also called *Panic*. By painting this enormous and unknown figure, Goya has conveyed an idea or a feeling that's impossible to describe.

The artist hasn't painted much detail.

The effect here appears rather brutal at first. There are marks of color and brushstrokes visible to the naked eye. The way he has painted it seems hurried, as if he hardly had time to prepare—just like the people he depicts. Goya has painted them with a quickness and lightness that captures their fragility and their haste. They are an anonymous, faceless crowd; we will never find out about them as individuals. But the colossus and the clouds that surround him are painted with much larger strokes. His strength is shown as much by the movement of the brush as by his size.

Was Goya painting a particular event?

Goya was probably alluding to the invasion of Spain by the French under Napoleon, though we can't tell whether the colossus represents the French threat to the Spanish people or Spain's guardian protecting the country. He admitted that he was painting a particular historical scene, without ever being absolutely clear about which one. The result was a general truth, a commentary on all wars. His painting could apply to any catastrophe anywhere, in any period.

Why is the subject of this painting so uncertain?

If Goya had wanted to paint an absolutely clear image, of course he could have done so. The uncertainty isn't due to any lack of skill on his part. On the contrary it is one of the painting's strengths. He has tackled how messy and illogical real life can be. Anyone, at any given moment, can be overtaken by overwhelming events. In their confusion Goya's figures are functioning instinctively; their sense of reason is eclipsed by their emotions. As a viewer, you can appreciate these feelings even better when you realize your own inability to know if the colossus is friend or foe. The only thing you can be sure of is fear.

Is Goya famous for dramatic subjects?

When he was younger, Goya painted lighthearted, happy scenes from everyday life as designs for tapestries commissioned by the royal family. He was also one of the most important portrait artists of his day. But the dramatic dimension we see in *The Colossus* was one of the cornerstones of his work. He was among the first to give such striking shape to abstract concepts such as fear. Of course before him artists painted invisible creatures such as gods, angels, or demons, but they all followed an unwritten code about how those creatures should look. A figure like the colossus was unprecedented. He is the embodiment of a nameless fear. Goya invented images that strike a chord with us at the deepest human level and, in that way, go far beyond any merely historical meaning. He painted things that words cannot name.

17 The Poor Poet

Painted 1838; oil on canvas; 36.2 x 44.6 cm
Neue Pinakothek, Munich, Germany
Carl Spitzweg
Born in Munich 1801; died in Munich 1885

He's got his clothes on in bed!

He has gone to bed with his clothes on because he is very, very cold. You can see the rooftops covered in snow through the window. This gentleman has put on a nightcap too. People don't wear them anymore, but they came in handy in those days when houses were badly heated.

Why is he in bed during the day?

It looks as though he hasn't got an armchair, a stool, or anything else to sit on. So, aside from sitting on the floor or standing up, if he wants to relax, he doesn't have much choice. If he's going to sit on the bed, he might as well get under the covers to keep warm.

The ceiling is sloping.

The man lives in a loft. It's not very large or comfortable. You can see the front door on the right-hand side, a huge stove on the left, and a little window at the back. To wash, he just uses a bowl, and he hangs his towel on a line. He hangs his coat on a nail in the wall.

There's an umbrella above the bed.

He fixed the umbrella there with a string because the roof is leaking. It would be better to have the roof mended, but he can't afford that. So, he has to make do with what he has. He's probably also trying not to hit his head on the handle of the umbrella.

The umbrella is ripped.

Yes, the old, patched-up umbrella has seen better days—it's ripped on one side and a spoke is sticking out on the other. But it still gets the job done. It must have been a while since the man bought anything new—the blanket is threadbare, and his jacket has a hole in the elbow.

Why doesn't he light the stove?

He needs wood to make a fire, and he doesn't have the money to buy any. He has already burned everything he can spare to keep himself warm; this is why the room doesn't have a chair, a table, or even a bed (you can see that his mattress is lying right on the floor). Almost everything he owns has gone up in smoke, and now there's no furniture left to burn.

What is he doing?

He is thinking about what he is going to write. The title of the painting tells us that he is a poet, and here you see him working. He has pieces of paper on his knee and is holding his quill pen in his mouth. An almost-empty inkwell sits beside him. He is counting syllables on the fingers of his other hand in order to compose a well-balanced poem. But maybe he's just crushing a flea.

Why is he so poor?

He is a writer and doesn't receive a regular wage from a regular job. He isn't employed by anyone. He has to find a journal that will publish at least one of his poems, but that doesn't happen very often. When he does manage to sell one, he doesn't receive much money for it; he's lucky if he earns enough for a meal.

Does he really only have one boot?

Even though you can only see one of them in the foreground, the other boot must be in a corner somewhere where the poet left it without paying as much attention to it as he did the first one. He just left the first one where it fell right next to the boot-pull. The boot-pull is the wooden thing on the ground: you jam your heel into the little opening and then pull your leg out of the boot. The artist shows us that the poet's mind is on loftier things than the details of everyday life. He is an artist, so his poems are far more important to him than whether or not he has put his boots away neatly.

His books are on the floor.

They are large, old, leather-bound books and he has piled them on the floor because he no longer has a bookcase. It's handier to have them like that anyway, because now he doesn't have to get out of bed to reach them. He can spend all his time reading, studying, and writing. His books are obviously precious to him; aside from his clothes they seem to be the only things he owns.

There are bundles of paper next to the stove.

They are manuscripts. He probably tossed them there when he came in; his walking stick is leaning against the wall nearby. He might use the papers to light his next fire; some of them are already inside the stove. Even if his poems aren't making him any money at least they can keep him warm.

Despite his situation he doesn't look desperate.

The artist hasn't really tried to convey the idea of misery. He's shown the outward signs of poverty—the leaky roof, the lack of furniture, the unlit stove—but those things are almost just decoration for the scene. It makes poverty look kind of romantic; Spitzweg shows it not as a cause of distress but as an inconvenience without any drawbacks. He focuses on how the poet is making the best of things. If the stove is cold, it's an ideal place to hang his hat. If there is no bookshelf, at least now he doesn't have to get out of bed to grab a book. If there is nothing left to burn, it's a good excuse to get rid of all those piles of paper.

Was it normal for poets to live like that in those days?

Most writers would work as teachers or in an office during the day and spend their free time on writing. So, even if their salaries were low, at least they they had a roof over their heads and food to eat. Spitzweg's character is clearly a dreamer: he thinks devoting himself fully to his art is a more noble pursuit. But of course Spitzweg knew being noble doesn't put food on the table; he was only able to devote himself to his painting thanks to an inheritance.

This painting's rather amusing; that seems rare.

Generally speaking, in the history of painting, amusing pictures are pretty rare. Paintings usually aim not to make people laugh but to teach them about religious or moral ideas or to impart knowledge. But beginning in the sixteenth century and increasing in frequency in the seventeenth century, Dutch painters took a somewhat humorous approach to subjects observed from everyday life like the chaos of a family party or the effects of gluttony or other displays of excess. But the artist's intentions here aren't satirical, and you sense a certain sympathy for his poet. He is happy to observe the poet from a distance without getting too close, the way you would look at an eccentric whose odd habits you nonetheless respect.

Was this painting a success?

This painting aroused the same sort of sympathy in the nineteenth century as it does with us today. Its charm comes partly from the fact that it combines everyday life with total idealism; the viewer sees the best of both. The sense of familiarity is pleasing because it lets you imagine yourself inside the picture, in the place of the poet, who is doing what he loves. The sense of idealism is also appealing because it suggests a softened and beautified version of harsh reality. Nothing appears too serious; problems will wait. To look at Spitzweg's poet you might think that it really is possible to live on dreams alone.

18 Rain, Steam and Speed— The Great Western Railway

Painted before 1844; oil on canvas; 91 x 122 cm
National Gallery, London, United Kingdom
Joseph Mallord William Turner
Born in London 1775; died in London 1851

You can hardly see anything.
The picture is full of fog. It's as if you are looking at the colors through gauze. You might feel a little lost, like it's difficult to get your bearings.

The road is very straight.
The structure in the painting is actually a viaduct. You can see the arched style a little better by looking at the second bridge on the left, which is farther away but clearer. On the large dark bridge in the foreground, you can make out the tracks and the arriving train. The far end of the train is still invisible, in the background of the painting.

There's a little boat on the left-hand side.
The boat is important because it makes it shows us that there is water below, not land. And since it is very small, it must be very far away. The landscape of the picture covers a large area.

It looks as if there is a fireball at the center of the painting.
The sun is reflected in the water and shining so hard that it makes everything look like it's on fire. Turner liked to paint that kind of light—so bright you think your eyes are going to burn. You can no longer distinguish anything in light so bright.

It's as if the painting has almost been washed away.
The rain, the steam, and the speed of the train make the countryside look hazy. The train is passing so quickly that you don't have time to see much of it. To achieve this blurry effect, Turner avoided painting outlines and used lots of different colors. The long strokes sweeping the sky give the illusion of rain. It's easy to imagine what the passengers might see from the windows of the train: vague shapes passing by, the wind blowing across the landscape, and drops of rain on the glass.

♦ ♦ ♦

Why did the painter choose this subject?
At the time the picture was painted, trains were a completely new invention. People had never imagined being able to travel like this, so quickly. It seemed magical. Everyone was full of admiration for the power and efficiency of the machines. Queen Victoria had inaugurated this very train line only two years before the painting was done. By choosing to paint a train, Turner depicted much more than just a means of transport—he was depicting the star of the age.

Why didn't the artist show the whole train?

The painting wouldn't have had the same sense of excitement if he had presented it in documentary fashion. Turner preferred to create an effect of surprise, to make it feel like you're really there at the moment when the train is passing: you're not sure what's happening, you hear a rumble, a cloud of steam appears, and suddenly, out of nowhere, a huge black shiny thing surges into view—it's the train.

The background is completely blurred.

The background is blurred for a number of reasons: the rain stops you from seeing very far, and, in those days, trains produced a lot of steam. The painting has a sense of mystery. You have no idea where the train has emerged from, and it appears to come straight out of the horizon, almost like it's coming out of the sky itself. This was a real train line that connected London and Bristol, England, and Turner knew it well; but, by painting it like this, he made it appear more impressionistic, almost supernatural.

Are there any people in the painting?

There are some people on the left of the bridge waving to the train as it goes by, there are other people on the little boat on the river; and there is a laborer on the right side of the painting working in a field. The fishermen in the boat and the laborer in the field represent an old-fashioned, traditional world; they are working much as men have since the Middle Ages. The train, on the other hand, with its noise and speed, belongs to the modern world, to the new industrial era. It is noisy and fast. The painting juxtaposes these two ways of life but doesn't set them up as opposites. The railway has become part of the landscape without impinging on the old way of life. Everyone continues on his or her way in a world full of changes.

How fast is the train going?

The year before the picture was painted, in 1843, a train set a record in Europe by going downhill at 75 miles per hour (120 kilometers per hour)—a considerable speed at the time. However, Turner has painted a rabbit escaping from the front of the train. Even though the rabbit is very small and slight in comparison with the huge machine, it still runs faster. Rabbits can only run about 43 miles per hour (70 kilometers per hour), so perhaps Turner was mocking the train or exploring the theme of pushing back limits in another way.

Was it common to see paintings of trains in those days?

No, people admired trains as technical achievements but didn't really consider them interesting subjects for paintings. To some artists trains were frightening and repulsive, and viewers liked paintings that told a story or showed tranquil landscapes where they could imagine walking or relaxing. So Turner's painting was exceptional and audacious. About twenty-five years later, however, Monet painted pictures of trains, too, after they had become popular in France.

Did Turner travel much?

He traveled all over England and also journeyed to Venice, Italy. During his trips he carefully wrote down in a notebook what the weather was like and how the changes in the colors of the sky related to the temperature. He closely followed changes in the weather, as you can see from his paintings. As an artist, Turner went to extraordinary lengths in his commitment to the truthful depiction of emotions and sensations. Once he went to sea at the height of a storm, in order to see how it felt to face such a situation. He had himself tied to the mast and stayed there for four hours.

Aside from the bridge, there aren't any lines in this painting.

The shape of the Maidenhead Viaduct, which had just been built in 1839, recalls one of the key areas of Turner's work: for several years he was professor of perspective at the Royal Academy of Arts. There he taught students to create the illusion of depth by, for example, using diagonal lines. The main element of this painting provides a perfect example of the technique, as well as offering Turner the chance to focus on the viaduct as a symbol of recent industrial progress.

The title of the painting is kind of strange.

Instead of naming the objects, such as the viaduct or the train, the title focuses on the elements that prevent those objects from being seen: rain, steam, and speed. The title does more than just describe the painting: it offers a description of how you view it. First, you can't see much of anything because of the rain, steam, and speed; then you find the subject—the railway. Beyond that, the title suggests three separate directions in the space: a descending vertical (rain), an ascending vertical (steam), and a horizontal crossing these two (speed). The success of the picture depends on the meeting of these opposing energies and on the feeling of contrast it evokes.

This painting feels ghostly.

The colors in the painting seem to float, as though they are detached from the earthly world. The artist combines robust observations with dreamlike unreality. You feel unsettled, as if you've drifted out of your depth. Turner loved to provoke that feeling. When he received visitors at his studio, he made them wait in a darkened room, and then, when their eyes had grown accustomed to the dark, he lead them to one of his paintings. The visitors would be blown away by the sumptuousness of the colors, like blind people who had suddenly regained their sight.

19 The Luncheon

Painted 1873–74; oil on canvas; 160 x 201 cm
Musée d'Orsay, Paris, France
Claude Monet
Born in Paris 1840; died at Giverny 1926

It's lovely weather!

Monet loved to paint sunlight. He has set up his painter's easel in the garden after lunch. The table hasn't yet been cleared and there are still some wine glasses, some bread, and some fruit. The pretty silver coffee pot is still there too, along with some cups. The coffee has probably gone cold by now. But there is no hurry.

Who is the child?

Jean, the painter's son, is playing in the shade. It's hard to see exactly what he is doing, but it looks like he is building something. He is concentrating with great effort and not paying any attention to the artist who is watching him. Both father and son absorbed in what they are doing. It's a very peaceful moment.

You can see some women in the background.

Everyone has left the table to take a little stroll. From time to time Jean's mother glances over, without disturbing him, to see that he's all right. The ladies won't walk too far away, though the fact that they are hidden by the flowers makes you realize that the garden is quite large.

Someone has left her hat behind.

Perhaps someone dropped it earlier, and then someone else found it and left it hanging there. Someone has also left her parasol behind as well, next to the basket on the wooden seat. Though it's very bright, it's probably not as hot as it was earlier in the day. A light breeze is gently lifting the ribbons on the hat.

There aren't any chairs around the table.

Perhaps the people only went outside for coffee and just sat on the bench. Or the artist might have left the chairs out of the painting so that it was not filled with too many lines and angles. In real life you need chairs, but you can do without them in a painting.

This painting doesn't have a story.

Monet wanted to show a moment when everything was pleasant and nothing special was happening. The people are simply strolling along, relaxing and chatting. If you were there, you'd find nothing out of the ordinary, just a simple life in which you felt agreeably relaxed. The painting isn't supposed to have a story.

♦ ♦ ♦

Since the painting is called *The Luncheon*, why don't we see people at the table?

It's true that the title doesn't exactly explain the picture. It doesn't show the meal, but it does convey what happened afterward. It seems unusual to put an empty table at the center of a painting. The people have scattered, but you have no doubt that they will gather around the table again. The table gives the impression that the family will reassemble there, even though they are elsewhere at the moment.

There's a lot of white in this painting.

Monet used the tablecloth to concentrate the light. Even though you can't see the sky, the painting is bursting with sunlight. The women's dresses in the background achieve the same effect, although to a lesser degree. But the amazing thing is that the whites are actually made up of other colors—blue, pink, and mauve. All the colors being reflected are mixed here, yet it always appears white.

Did Monet really paint in the garden?

Monet believed things should be painted where they were, so if he wanted to paint a view of a garden, he would paint it in the garden. Before then, it was more common to work in a studio, regardless of the subject of the painting. Of course, working in a studio allowed the artist the freedom to work at any time of day or night, but the light in a studio was quite different from the light outdoors. Monet preferred to observe things *in situ*—in nature—in order to paint them as they really were.

What difference does painting outside make?

Painting outside makes a huge difference to a painter's methods. Anything that moves can be a distraction. Daylight doesn't last, and the weather changes. If a painter starts painting in nice weather, for example, and then the sky turned cloudy and grey, she would have to wait for the colors and the light she first saw to reappear. Everything changes quickly and a painter must get the paint down without dawdling—otherwise the moment is lost, and the thing he or she was painting doesn't exist any more. A certain ray of light between two clouds might suddenly disappear when the clouds darken, and then it's gone forever.

Did Monet paint very quickly?

Monet certainly would have liked to have painted as swiftly as things—a shifting cloud, a flying ribbon, a floating reflection—changed around him, but that would have been impossible. He spent a lot of time just observing things, training his eyes. It's actually incredibly difficult to give the impression in a painting that everything has been captured on canvas in an instant. He would sometimes spend a long time on a single brushstroke.

Why did the artist paint such vague shapes?

When we look at things, most of the time we only have a general image of them. For example, we can't really see every leaf on a tree in all its detail. We see shapes and colors in general. This effect is what Monet wanted to show. By not painting exact outlines he remained true to what he saw.

It's easier to do vague shapes than to draw properly.

No, it's just a different way of working. Drawing in minute detail allows a painter to fully depict an object. Take the rose on the table, for instance: Monet could have shown all its details and captured all the subtle nuances of color in its petals and leaves. However, he chose to paint it as it appears after a casual glance and not how it "really" is. The rose simply becomes a colorful shape and nothing more. And that is Monet's talent: capturing the essence of how something appears when it is only glimpsed.

Did other painters paint outdoors?

Monet was one of the first to work outside regularly, but others—including his friends Sisley, Renoir, and Pissarro—did so too. These artists made the most of a new invention: paint in tubes, which was easily transportable. And people were just discovering the railways then. From a train landscapes appeared blurred, and you didn't have time to see every detail. Monet and the others captured these new sensations.

Why is Monet called an Impressionist?

At first, the name "Impressionist" was a joke. In 1874 Monet exhibited a painting called *Impression, Sunrise*, in which all you could see were very vague shapes. This is where the term "Impressionist" came from. Many people felt that this painting proved that Monet couldn't paint and that this was a botched or hurried job. (In those days "impression" also meant "sketch.") No one realized that Monet would change painting forever and that in future artists would focus on such tiny fragile, fleeting impressions.

Now everybody loves Impressionist paintings.

These paintings weren't very popular at the time they were first painted. The public preferred paintings of lofty subjects, such as spectacular scenery or distinguished people, or paintings that told a story. But now we find it somewhat reassuring to look at paintings that capture a moment from everyday life. Everyone has experienced a sunny day, a family lunch, or a walk. When you see a painting like this, even for the first time, it's immediately familiar. There is nothing to understand, you don't feel ignorant or disoriented, and you feel at ease.

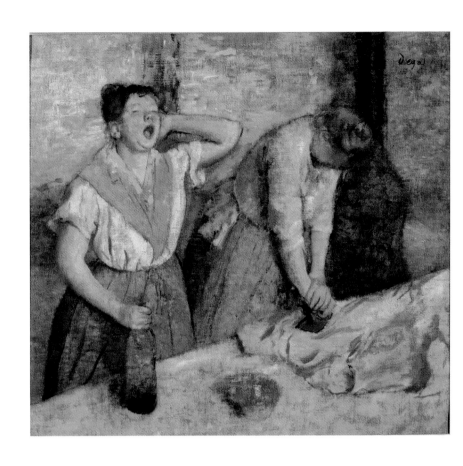

20 Women Ironing

Painted about 1884–86; oil on canvas; 76 x 81 cm
Musée d'Orsay, Paris, France
Edgar Degas
Born in Paris 1834; died in Paris 1917

What are these women doing?
They are doing their job—ironing. They work in a laundry.

Don't they have a machine to do the ironing?
At the time when this picture was painted, electric irons hadn't been invented yet and everything had to be done by hand. You had to heat the irons on the stove (that's the dark shape in the background), and when one was hot enough to use, you had to wrap the handle in a cloth so you wouldn't burn yourself before you could pick it up. It was important to heat several irons at the same time, so as soon as one cooled down, it could be swapped for a nice hot one.

One of the women is yawning.
She's tired after working many long hours and is taking a quick break. She's got backache and her neck is stiff from having been bent over all day. The room is terribly hot, and the air must be very stuffy by the stove.

Why is she holding a bottle?
Even though it looks like she's going to drink from it, she will actually use the water to moisten the linen. If the fabric is too dry, sprinkling a little water on it will make it easier to iron. She's probably about to refill her little red bowl.

The one who is ironing is pressing really hard.
At that time clothes weren't made from synthetic fabric. The shirt she is ironing was probably of cotton or linen, and very stiff. To remove all the wrinkles she would have had to use all her weight, pressing down with both hands. And the iron would have been very heavy (some weighed as much as six pounds), so it wouldn't slide across the fabric easily and would have been difficult to maneuver.

♦ ♦ ♦

They aren't very well dressed.
They are not wealthy so their clothes are modest, made of coarse fabric. But the orange and pink colors of their dresses are pretty and feminine; together they create a sense of warmth that is key to creating the picture's atmosphere.

Did these women ask the artist to paint their portrait?
Strictly speaking, this painting isn't really a portrait. You can't see their faces very clearly and you don't know their names. But these women would have been far too poor anyway to afford to commission a painting. By this point at the end of the nineteenth century, a painter like Degas didn't have to solely rely on commissions; he could choose his own subjects.

So why did Degas paint them?

Degas liked painting bodies; he liked painting the particular way people would stand in any given circumstance or to do a certain task. He probably observed the women closely while they were ironing, and had the idea to capture some of their poses. At the time it was unusual for paintings to show ordinary people doing everyday tasks.

Why aren't they looking at us?

Degas painted people without making them pose. It looks as though they aren't even aware the painter is there. They have remained natural and aren't worried about how elegant or graceful they look.

He must have worked very quickly to have been able to paint without them noticing.

The scene looks as though it was captured as it happened, but actually it would have taken a lot of preparation. Just as a photographer or a reporter might film his subjects for days, Degas wrote notes about ironing techniques and observed the precise gestures that the women used. At first perhaps they would have been intimidated by his presence, but as soon as they became absorbed in their work it's likely they forgot all about him. Later, Degas would have done many studies and sketches. The painting itself would have been the last stage after a lot of hard work.

Did Degas paint people in other professions?

He often painted dancers. He used to watch them rehearsing, repeating the same movement thousands of times; they are featured in many of his paintings. He painted them while they were resting, when they had a sore foot or when they were retying their shoes. Degas loved to show the ways that the human body can be as expressive and revealing as a face, such as the way a dancer holds her back, the way she lowers her body without bending at the knee.

Why doesn't this painting look finished?

Many of Degas's works have this vaguely unfinished feeling. He was bored by little details and considered them superfluous and petty. It was important to him that his images should be full of movement and not appear fixed—he admitted he was always in a hurry. He was constantly captivated by gestures and attached particular significance to them. This painting has a powerful atmosphere—you almost feel as if you are in the room with them in the stifling heat.

Why doesn't the paint cover the whole canvas?

In several places you can see the canvas through the paint, almost if the paint isn't sticking to it properly. But in fact Degas has used this technique as the best way to interpret his subject. These women's jobs dealt with fabric, so he emphasized the presence of the canvas by leaving it visible in spots. He usually preferred very fine canvases but for this painting he chose a very coarse one because it is depicting toil and misery. In this way the reality of the material becomes associated with the image, and it immediately impresses itself upon our minds. The colors in the painting could have been light and fluid; instead they are lumpy and dry. Just looking at it makes you feel thirsty and your arms tired, just like these women.

Degas doesn't show much.

He is happy just to hint. We don't really know how many piles of washing they still have to get through, but the shirt overflowing the table makes it clear that it's hard work and there is no end in sight. And we know that the yawning woman will probably quickly return to her work: notice the way the triangle of her scarf links her to the outline of the woman who is still ironing.

Why did Degas paint two women?

Their poses are complementary: it could almost be the same person painted twice. By painting two women he can actually show two successive moments of the same action. One woman is hunched over the fabric and the other is stretched out. Looking at them one after the other you understand that they represent two stages of a breath, inhalation and exhalation. You can sympathize with how tired they must be.

Did the public like Degas's paintings?

Many people were shocked by his subject matter and found it vulgar. People were also shocked by the way he showed women without decorum. Eventually viewers came to appreciate the truth of his paintings, which were full of the realities of modern life, far removed from the idealized tales of immortal Greek and Roman heroes that were popular at that time. These situations were similar to the narratives in the contemporary novels of Émile Zola.

21 The Bedroom

Painted October 1888. Oil on canvas; 72 x 90 cm
Van Gogh Museum, Amsterdam, The Netherlands
Vincent van Gogh
Born at Groot Zunder, Brabant 1853; died at Auvers-sur-Oise 1890

Whose bedroom is it?

The bedroom belongs to the artist, Vincent van Gogh. When he painted it, he was living in Arles, a town in Provence in the south of France.

It's a very tidy bedroom.

By painting this bedroom where everything is in its place, van Gogh is showing that he has now decided to take care of himself and to organize his life properly. Up until the point when he painted this, he had mainly lived in inns and hadn't really settled down anywhere.

The colors are pretty.

The weather in Holland, where van Gogh was born, was not always good, so he came to Provence in search of sunshine. He probably loved having a bedroom so full of light and bursting with colors. You can't see much through the window, but you can sense that there is a great deal of light.

There isn't much furniture.

Vincent was very poor so he only had the essentials, and what he had was very plain, simple, wooden furniture. Of course there is a bed, and there are also two chairs, in case someone comes to visit. In those days there were no bathrooms: to wash, he used a jug of water and a bowl on the bedside table. His towel is close by, hanging from a nail next to the mirror.

There are paintings on the walls.

Vincent spent all his time painting. It was the thing he most loved in the whole world. For him it was unthinkable to live in a place without paintings, so he hung his own work on the walls. On the right-hand side there are two portraits of friends and underneath those are drawings you can tell were done on paper. On the back wall he has a landscape. These represent all the different styles of his work.

♦ ♦ ♦

Why are his belongings in pairs?

There are two chairs, two pillows, two portraits on the wall, two drawings, and even two doors. He didn't share the bedroom with anyone, but perhaps multiplying everything by two made him feel less lonely.

The walls seem a bit uneven.

The far wall isn't very straight. The bedroom was in a corner of the house that leaned over at a bit of an angle. In another picture, *The Yellow House*, van Gogh painted the house from the outside, and in that picture you can clearly see how uneven the walls are.

There's nothing to suggest it's a painter's bedroom.

There is no way of knowing that it's an artist's bedroom because his materials are not on display. None of his supplies have been left out, not even a stray box or paintbrush. Van Gogh used to work outside for many hours every day (you can see his jackets and his straw hat at the end of the room), but this room is meant for relaxation. In here he could forget his work, make himself comfortable, and sleep peacefully. He wanted this painting to convey that idea of restfulness.

There aren't many different colors.

Van Gogh tried to make his paintings as intense and as full of impact as possible so he chose only contrasting colors, such as blue and orange and green and red, which gave force to his painting. They were like a concentration of energy. He ignored any shadows that might have diminished the vibrancy of his paintings. The color of the frame was also intended to play a role: he wanted a completely white frame to counterbalance the liveliness of the picture.

It's a very simple picture.

The objects shown are unexceptional and the colors, despite being bright, are flat, without any subtlety of tones. Van Gogh wanted his paintings to be easy to understand. The outlines of the objects are easy to follow—he generally used thick lines. But on the inside, things are far from simple: the paint is very thick and the brushstrokes are laid on top of each other. The furniture is also arranged strangely: both the doors are blocked, one by a chair and the other by the bed. It's probably not that easy to live here.

We notice the bed first.

At the far end of the room the walls lean in toward one another quite steeply. This effect exaggerates the size of the room and makes the bed seem enormous and the floor seem to rise upward. If you imagine the room without the red blanket, everything seems to crumble and slide toward the floor. The triangle of red blanket seems to pin the surface of the painting in place. As long as it is there, everything stays in balance. The red color is warm and makes the blanket seem comforting. There is a sense of real tension in the painting: it almost seems like the bed could sink like a ship. For the moment however, it is still afloat.

Is it true that van Gogh was crazy?

He was anxious and psychologically fragile, and he suffered a great deal. During the time that he was alive, doctors didn't know how to properly treat mental and emotional problems. But when he painted, he knew exactly what he wanted to do and why. In the hundreds of letters he wrote, particularly the ones addressed to his brother Theo, he gives a lucid commentary on his work. He was exceptionally sensitive and intelligent.

Van Gogh's paintings are unlike anyone else's.

They are brash and violent, in some ways like the artist himself. But van Gogh was also very cultured, and he appreciated traditional painting as well as the work of his contemporaries. Like other artists at that time, he was interested in Japanese prints and looked to them as inspiration for his bold use of colors and simple shapes.

Did people like his paintings?

People found them frightening, which is what you would feel if someone was yelling nonsense at you. But very few people actually saw van Gogh's paintings. As he completed each painting, he sent them to his brother Theo in Paris. When he died in 1890, he had only ever sold one painting. He was in despair about this, but he never pandered to public taste to try and make money. He never compromised his artistic vision.

How did van Gogh become so famous?

People only began to appreciate the impact of his work after he died. He was terribly lonely and finally committed suicide, penniless and still unknown to the world. Many people find the contrast between the sadness of his life and the exuberance of his art fascinating. His life story gives his art a dramatic, almost sacred dimension; our current feelings about him go beyond just the things that he painted.

Why don't we see his signature?

This painting doesn't have a signature. In the nineteenth century artists did usually sign their work, but van Gogh was such a perfectionist that he often thought of his paintings as simple studies and didn't automatically sign everything. He didn't think his paintings were worth it. When he did sign his work he wrote his first name, which was more intimate than an ordinary signature, almost friendly. That's why he's often referred to as "Vincent" rather than "van Gogh."

22 The Birthday

Painted 1915; oil on card; 80.6 x 99.7 cm
Museum of Modern Art, New York, United States of America
Marc Chagall
Born at Vitebsk 1887; died Saint-Paul-de-Vence 1985

They're flying!

These people are flying because they are in love. The painting is of the artist himself, Marc Chagall, who has just been reunited with his fiancée, Bella, after a long time apart. They are so happy that they are want to run and jump, and they feel as light as birds. Here they are, kissing each other.

Why doesn't he have arms?

In real life, he definitely would have scooped her up in his arms. But the painting expresses what he feels: he didn't just want to hug Bella in his arms, he wanted to envelop her with his whole body and wrap himself around her.

She's holding a bunch of flowers.

He has given these flowers to her for her birthday. He must have come up behind her before she had a chance to turn around, to take her by surprise. He's so deliriously happy that he doesn't know whether he's coming or going, so his head is shown back to front.

There aren't any birthday candles.

The scene takes place in Vitebsk, the village in Russia where they were born. In Russia it's not traditional to have candles on a birthday cake. But the cake is ready, on the red table with the pretty blue tablecloth. All they have to do is slice it and serve it.

The house is very colorful.

There aren't many things in the room and the things they do have aren't very luxurious, but the bright colors—especially the red floor—give the impression that the room is full. Bella's shawls hang on the walls and, with their patterns of little flowers and geometric shapes, liven up the room. This painting is a feast for the eyes.

So the artist painted himself.

Yes, this painting is a self-portrait even though it isn't a very accurate one. It doesn't have to be. Because he is with Bella, we know it's definitely Chagall himself.

♦ ♦ ♦

What is outside the window?

Beyond the table you can see a village street and a church, but it's far too cold in Russia to open the whole window. Notice how at the top of the window it's dark outside, but at the bottom of the window, you can see clearly in broad daylight. Chagall liked to mix dreamlike elements with realistic details in his paintings.

The table doesn't have enough legs to support it.
Everyone knows tables need to have at least four legs, and of course Chagall knew that. However, he only painted what was necessary to understand the picture. Anything can happen in this painting. The same impossible logic explains why he doesn't have arms and why Bella needs only one hand to hold her flowers.

The people are very big compared to everything else.
The figures are larger because the story of the painting is about them. Everything else is just there to set the scene. Bella looks even bigger than Chagall; this shows how much she means to him. There is nothing more important in the whole world to him than her. By painting in this style, Chagall was working in the tradition of medieval painters who depicted people not according to their actual size but according to their level of importance.

Why does the furniture look like it's falling over?
The table and the black stool are seen from above, the way the people in the painting see them. They see them like that because they are flying. We, standing in front of the picture, see the shawls on the walls, the two windows, and the flowers straight on. Chagall pulls us into the image by combining these two points of view—ours outside the painting and the people's inside it.

Everything is a bit lopsided.
This painting isn't meant to be an accurate snapshot of everyday life. Chagall painted as though he were telling a fairy story or fable. The Jewish culture he was born and grew up in is full of fanciful stories. In Hassidic legends, for example, people fly, trees laugh, and there are fiddlers on the rooftops. Chagall never forgot these stories. Their influence is central to his work.

Sometimes the grey swallows up the other colors.
There is grey around the stool and under the table; there is a loop of grey under Chagall's feet; and the front of Bella's dress is like a cloud melting the black fabric. The artist maintains a balance: he draws some objects very clearly and then he suddenly appears to have gotten bored. He let his paintbrush wander across the painting. The shapes look unrealistic, almost as if the colors themselves were out of control, doing what they want on their own.

It feels as if you're in a fairy tale.

Chagall painted as though life was a fairy tale, and, at the time, that's just how his love affair with Bella must have felt. But the painting is not just about his personal happiness. He shows a world in constant change because, in Judaism, divine creation is considered a never-ending process. To paint a fixed world would have been to deny the creative power of God. Chagall didn't want to freeze the world in his paintings; on the contrary, he wanted his paintings to be part of its development.

Did Chagall explain his paintings?

Without going into any technical details, Chagall described in his memoirs numerous moments that are echoed in his paintings. He said he liked to work like a cobbler. Cobblers attach shoe soles by turning the shoe in their hand, and that is how Chagall liked to paint—in every direction.

Did Chagall often paint scenes from his own life?

Yes, Chagall painted people he knew and places he liked. In that sense his paintings are autobiographical. But he also painted many other subjects, especially scenes from the Bible. His paintings always have a somewhat marvelous quality to them; he wanted to convey the idea that no matter how much suffering there is in the world, it is still full of magic.

Did Chagall always live in Russia?

When he was twenty-three, he went to France to study modern painting and returned to Russia a few years later to marry Bella, which is when he painted this picture. After that he mainly lived in France, aside from a brief time in the United States as a refugee during World War II. In 1937 he officially became a French citizen, but he always remained a Russian at heart.

23 The Mechanic

Painted 1920; oil on canvas; 115.5 x 88.3 cm
National Gallery of Art, Ottawa, Canada
Fernand Leger
Born at Argentan 1881; died at Gif-sur-Yvette 1955

It's a sailor!
You can tell it's a sailor right away because he has a tattoo of an anchor on his arm. Tattoos are drawn with ink under the skin and can't be removed. He's a real sailor; he's not pretending.

He's very muscular.
He doesn't go to sea just for the fun of it. He's a mechanic, and he works hard, so he has to be strong. The painter has emphasized his arms, giving him big shoulders and enormous forearms and hands.

He's smoking.
He's taking a moment to relax; he doesn't have anything particular to do. His cigarette is giving off a lot of smoke—in fact, it looks more like a chimney. There's far too much for a single cigarette. Maybe it's suggesting that the sailor smokes too much.

He's wearing hair gel.
In those days it was known as "brilliantine." Men put it on their hair to make it shiny and hold it in place. He's definitely used some because his hair looks very neat. It must be his day off, and he's made himself look good.

He's wearing little rings.
The rings look very small on his big hand. Maybe they were a present from someone special or a souvenir. Maybe he is wearing them so he has them ready to give as presents, just in case.

There are all kinds of shapes behind him.
Those shapes represent the kind of world he lives in—he's surrounded by pieces of iron, metal, pipes, bolts, and screws. He knows how everything works and how to maintain the machines.

He looks like a strong man.
He's a mechanic. His body works as smoothly as the machines he operates. He is in harmony with them. You could say that he has muscles of steel.

There aren't many colors.
There aren't many colors in this painting, but the few colors the artist has used are very strong. The way the colors spread over the canvas creates contrasts: black/white, yellow/black, like lights going on and off. They are not there to help

us to recognize specific objects being depicted: they add rhythm to the painting. The colors in the background are flat with no shading in order to emphasize the solidity of the figure in the foreground.

Why aren't there actual objects behind the mechanic?

The painter wanted to create a general impression, not show a particular place or set of objects. Looking at this painting you don't see dust, grease, or noise. The artist has kept only the simplest lines and smoothest surfaces. And he has placed them one on top of another, showing them all in relation to and in opposition to one another: curves and straight lines, horizontals and verticals, thin and thick stripes of color. The more you look at the picture, the more architectural it appears.

Everything in this painting is stiff.

Fernand Leger chose shapes that suggest plain-colored goods that have been mass-produced in factories from industrial materials. The painting conveys the mechanical world, a world of staccato movements, clear instructions, total precision, and perfect regularity. It shows a man who is living in the machine age and who shares the machines' qualities.

Why didn't the artist show a real place?

If we were able to recognize a certain port, road, boat, or machine, the artist would have been creating something more akin to a landscape or a documentary. That wasn't his aim: his painting isn't about anyone in particular and it isn't a portrait. Leger is showing a general category of men. This painting could be applicable to any mechanic on any boat.

He's got arms like Popeye!

The Popeye character was also a sailor, so, yes, they look a bit alike. Both of them have unrealistic arms: the muscles aren't in the right places at all. This emphasis on their exceptional strength sets them apart from ordinary people. In fact the Popeye character was created around the same time as Leger was painting: he first appeared in an American comic in 1929. Popeye and this mechanic are from exactly the same generation.

The mechanic looks bored.

He doesn't really have any expression at all. He is unruffled and unflappable. Nothing can change his features; they are made of rigid elements. His forehead is like an arc of metal following the upper edge of his eyebrows. The artist wasn't trying to convey emotions; he was trying to get at the spirit of an age. In 1924 he used the newly developed cinema technology to make a movie without a plot, entitled *Mechanical Ballet*.

Why is his head in profile but his shoulders are facing forward?

Showing his face in profile clearly delineates the character and allows you to see the main features (the shape of his nose and his chin) without being distracted by his expression. Showing the width of his shoulders emphasizes their muscular strength and gives you a sense of the physical reality of his body. Leger's technique here is following a very ancient tradition: the Egyptians also used to paint people in this way. It makes the painting clear and efficient.

It looks more like a robot than a man.

This is definitely a man, but he is well adapted to the world of robots. He is made up of the very same shapes he works with in his day-to-day life. Leger believed that his paintings should be accessible to people who worked in factories. He wanted his paintings to reflect ordinary things that ordinary workers would recognize from their own lives—not scenes of castles, silk, or gold, but bold lines and real colors. His lines and shapes make a social statement here as well as an aesthetic one.

Did Leger do other paintings like this one?

Yes, for him it was essential to pay homage to the masses, who were making industrial progress possible. His *Mechanic* is in profile, like a Roman emperor on a coin or the portrait of a Renaissance prince. By painting him like this, Leger ennobled the humble worker, showing him as the true hero of modern times, who would create a magnificently efficient and harmonious society, a world where man is served by machines and freed from the shackles of the past. After World War I, this was the dream of the humanists, who believed deeply in a better, happier, and more just world.

24 Composition with Red, Yellow and Blue

Painted 1930; oil on canvas; 45 x 45 cm
Kunsthaus, Zurich, Switzerland
Pieter Cornelis Mondriaan Mondrian
Born at Amersfoort 1872; died in New York 1944

There's almost nothing to see in this painting.

Sometimes artists paint things that are more complicated than everyday life: an elegant portrait, a huge landscape, or even a dragon. But sometimes an artist prefers to show the world simpler than it is in real life. That's what Mondrian does.

Does this painting represent anything?

It doesn't represent anything in particular. It invites us to imagine all kinds of possibilities. The artist didn't want to show a ready-made object, so he simply painted everything needed to create something. It's like a game: with the different pieces and a palette of colors, you can invent whatever you want.

Perhaps the artist didn't know how to paint anything else.

Mondrian was perfectly able to paint "normally," and he did so for many years. But that wasn't enough for him; he wanted to do something more. Little by little he took out the details that annoyed him or didn't seem useful. Eventually there was nothing left but straight lines and three colors. And he was happy with that.

Did he draw it with a ruler?

Yes, this was very carefully planned work that he had thought about for a long time. He measured out his canvas using strips of tracing paper to decide where to put the lines. Then he drew them in with charcoal and painted over them.

Red, blue, and yellow: why did he paint those three colors?

These three colors are the minimum. By combining them you can create any other color in the rainbow: green, purple, orange, and all the shades in between. But it is impossible to make any of them individually—that's why they're called the primary colors.

There is also black and white.

Without black and white it's impossible to lighten or darken colors. The black lines organize the picture, limiting the spaces, making them shorter, taller, broader, or narrower. The white spaces give the impression of emptiness, light, and air. The squares filled with color are full of energy. For example, red can evoke fire or blood or a sunset. The black lines control the structure of the painting by not letting anything overflow.

Lines and colors replace places and people in this painting.

The artist is establishing a dialogue, making links between lines and colors. The red square, for example, looks so strong and heavy that you can imagine it overflowing beyond the painting—it's not even held in by a black border. But the smaller horizontal lines in the top left and bottom right are wider than the others and look as though they've been put there to hold the red square in place. Without these robust little lines, who knows where the color might end up!

Why isn't there a black outline around the whole painting?

If there were a border, the painting would be enclosed. Mondrian doesn't imprison his colors; he presents them to us as if they are suspended, without limiting our field of vision. The doors are always open so that you can enter the painting, explore it, and slip out again whenever you want. After you've studied this painting for a while, it's possible that you will see the rest of the world differently. In a way the painting is training you to see more clearly.

It's like an apartment, with walls, rooms, and different colors.

An architectural plan is indispensable for determining what you want to be built. According to Mondrian, painting provided a model of reason and stability to our lives. In this way, the painting and a building plan have something in common.

It could represent the facade of a building.

Looking at this painting, it's easy to imagine a building that's being knocked down, where whole bare walls reveal rooms that don't exist any more. From what is left of the colors on the walls you can guess where the furniture used to stand or whether it was a bedroom or a sitting room. Whole lives have been reduced to a few rectangles. This kind of simplicity inspired Mondrian.

It could also be a plan of a city with its streets and avenues.

There is nothing to indicate scale or size. Maybe you can imagine seeing these shapes from a bird's-eye view. Years after painting many pictures in this style, Mondrian traveled to the United States and fell in love with New York. The city itself is arranged like one of his paintings—it's a network of lines crisscrossing each other at right angles. This world perfectly corresponded to his own.

All Mondrian's paintings look the same.

His paintings are based on the same principles, but the ratios of color and the proportions differ. In some paintings, white fills almost all of the space, and the work seems peaceful and light. In others the lines are closer together, like prison bars, making the work so oppressive that you feel like you might want to run away from it. With the simplest of means Mondrian suggests an incredibly rich range of emotions. He is like a composer who can create an infinite variety of tunes using only seven notes. After all, this painting is called a "composition."

A painting like that looks easy to do.

Technically, it wouldn't be difficult. The difficulty comes from the levels of the painting's meanings. Anyone can imitate this kind of painting, but no one can go back in time and live Mondrian's life over again. It took him many years to develop this style. Today, when you stand in front of one of his paintings, it is much more than an apparently simple image: it's the sum of all his ideas. The details of his life led him, on that one day, to create a work like this. This is not just a one-time-only event. In a way, this painting is his whole life.

The painting looks almost mechanical.

The geometry of the design gives a mechanical impression, especially if you look at it too quickly. It can seem rigid at first, but when you look closer, you can see more than austerity. The brushstrokes are visible in the black lines and some of them even appear to wobble a little. It feels a little surprising to get a sense of the vulnerability of the artist's hand. And you discover that the lines aren't systematically painted one over the other—they're actually crisscrossing each other. Mondrian weaves them together like a web. It gives the impression that the fibers of the canvas itself magnified, as if seen through a microscope, and you suddenly discover the hidden support of the painting.

Was it easy for Mondrian to sell his paintings?

A painting like this is a sort of mental exercise, and it didn't appeal to many people at first. But even in the face of indifference from the art-buying public, Mondrian continued to paint like this because he had to be true to himself and his artistic vision of the world. To support himself he painted pictures of flowers that sold very well. These paintings allowed him to preserve his own unique world, a world of straight lines and pure color. Today that is the work for which he is remembered and admired and respected. The flowers that enabled him to live are almost forgotten.

All kinds of objects from daily life seem like aspects of Mondrian's paintings.

Not only did his work influence generations of other painters, but they also influenced the everyday world we live in. More than half a century after his death, we still see the effects everywhere: in interior decoration, in furniture design, in graphic art, in magazines, in advertising, and in fashion. His paintings simultaneously express a moral absolute and a structural stability. The ideas in his paintings touch our lives perhaps without our realizing it. The logo for L'Oreal's Studio Line range of hair products, for example, is clearly based on Mondrian's shapes, and, underneath that, on his principles as well. Hair gel or shampoo will sell better if the consumer automatically associates it with ideas of purity, dynamism, and creativity. Suddenly, with these products, everything is possible: discipline and rhythm, freedom of combinations, and the certainty of efficiency.

25 **Weeping Woman**

Painted 26 October 1937; oil on canvas; 60 x 49 cm
Tate Modern, London, England
Pablo Picasso
Born Malaga 1881; died Mougins 1973

It's a face in a jigsaw!

The face is in small pieces, but the shapes are a lot less regular than in a jigsaw. It looks as if the pieces were carelessly made and some of them might not even be in the right places.

Everything is pointy.

The world seems pointy because the woman here is in pain. Everything is troubling her. The shapes are jagged and sharp. It's easy to tell that this woman is suffering.

She has a funny ear.

Her earring is not fixed to her ear: it's pinching the middle of it. It must be painful. With her ear closed like that, it must also be hard to hear. She is in so much pain that she isn't aware of what is going on around her. No one can even say anything to console her because she wouldn't be able to hear it.

She's wearing a red hat.

She's an elegant lady; she is well dressed and has neatly styled hair. Perhaps she has just arrived home and hasn't had time to take off her hat or perhaps she is getting ready to go out. But she's been interrupted. With that hat, Picasso shows that something unexpected has happened. She does not usually look like this. This isn't her normal state of mind.

What is she holding in her hand?

She is probably holding a handkerchief. Perhaps the points touching her eyes are its corners. Her tears hang as heavy drops in her eyes. The fabric is all scrunched up in her hand, and she has been chewing at it. She doesn't know what to do.

She's broken.

Her face is disfigured from crying. She isn't actually physically broken, but she feels broken inside. She is horribly unhappy and what you see in the painting is what she feels: everything has gone wrong, nothing helps, and not even the handkerchief can wipe away her tears.

Why is her face painted with those colors?

The colors in this painting are like the colors skin turns when it has been hit and forms a bruise. Over time it changes from blue and purple to green and yellow. This woman hasn't been physically beaten, but she is suffering greatly and she feels as if she's been beaten black and blue. Her pain is so violent that it makes her feel physically ill. The colors suggest that her sadness is not isolated; it's like she has received blow after blow. Even if the situation starts to improve, it's likely to start all over again.

Part of her face is all white.

The whiteness shows that she is pale. This is like a literal depiction of the phrase "as white as a sheet." She is so weak that she probably feels like there's no blood in her veins at all.

Real people don't look like that.

Picasso didn't want to paint how she looked. He wanted to paint how she felt. There is often a big gap between how you look and how you actually feel. When you pass people in the street, you can't necessarily tell how they are feeling, what's worrying them, what makes them laugh or cry. It was exactly those invisible feelings that Picasso wanted to capture. He made people transparent.

Picasso has completely demolished her face.

No, her pain has demolished her face, and Picasso has found a way to bring her pain into the light of day. He's not just making his model look ugly for the fun of it, to make her look unrecognizable. There's no cruelty on the artist's part here.

It's a complicated painting.

It may seem complicated at first, but Picasso is trying to show things very directly. We all use expressions like "burst into tears" or "fall to pieces." We know that they are just expressions, not descriptions of something that has actually happened. But Picasso takes these phrases to their logical conclusion and actually paints them.

Did the woman really exist?

Yes, this woman lived with Picasso. She was the photographer Dora Marr. She was very upset when her father died, and the face this beautiful woman made when she cried must have fascinated the painter. But the the painting is not named after her; it is called *Weeping Woman*. Picasso didn't think of this painting as a portrait. From one specific person, he created a type of face in which each human being can recognize his or her own pain.

This painting is like a reflection in a broken mirror.

Yes, the idea of a broken mirror reinforces the sense of pain. Shards of mirror are jagged and sharp. In the past painters tried to hold a mirror up to nature, assuming that it was possible to present a perfect imitation of the visible world, like a photograph. In his own style Picasso is saying that when the world seems to be falling apart, the mirror must be in pieces, too. An artist must not try to paint a harmony where there is none.

This painting is unpleasant to look at.

Pain is not pleasant, and this painting of pain is not pleasant either. Before Picasso, people painted suffering almost in an idealized way. The world in other paintings was sometimes cruel, yes, but it almost doesn't matter if it is other people's suffering. Picasso was one of the first artists to paint suffering from the inside. We recognize the world he shows us in his paintings because we've felt these emotions, too. If the painting is shocking it's because suffering itself is shocking. We are afraid of seeing it.

Could Picasso have painted a weeping man?

He could have if he had wanted to, but Dora Marr was part of his life and she was his model for this painting. But the fact that she is a woman adds an interesting element to this painting: there is something ridiculous about her pain. Her nice hair and earrings—all the things that usually make a woman appear elegant—now conspire to make her look laughable or, worse, grotesque. A woman crying can be a tender sight, but when she has make-up running down her cheeks, she can feel even more humiliated because now she has the face of a sad clown.

Why paint a picture that people will find ugly?

Picasso didn't paint to please people. He painted for himself, because he felt the need to express something through painting. If people were moved by his paintings and understood what he was trying to express, that was good, but it wasn't his primary aim. Sometimes it's not helpful to describe a painting as just being beautiful or ugly; in this case the painting wouldn't be meant to decorate a room and make it look pretty. This painting is not an ornament but an instrument of the truth. Picasso unmasks suffering and shows how it rips people to shreds.

26 Number 3, Tiger

Painted 1949; oil and metallic enamel on canvas mounted on fiberboard;
157.4 x 94.2 cm
Hirshhorn Museum and Sculpture Garden, Smithsonian Institution,
Washington, DC, United States of America
Jackson Pollock
Born at Cody, Wyoming 1912; died at Springs, Long Island 1956

It's just a scribble.

Yes, but it's an immense scribble. It's rare to see such a big one.

Did a painter really do this?

Yes, Jackson Pollock really was an artist. He was very good at drawing, but he preferred to paint like this because it was the best way he found to express what he wanted to say.

There's nothing to see in this painting.

It seems muddled at first, but nevertheless you can start to make out shapes and colors. After a while, you begin to realize that this is very complicated.

What could it be?

We don't know, and we may never find out. Nothing is certain. Perhaps that's just what the painter wanted to say: here is something that you can't name and you can't understand. Everything is confused. The painting raises questions without answering them.

There are colors everywhere.

These colors seem to have a life of their own, entwining each other like pieces of string without ever mingling. The lines pass over each other, thicken, and become so fine that they look like they could break. There are probably plenty of colors underneath it all that you can't quite make out. There are just so many! The painter included almost every color he could.

Looking at it too long makes you dizzy.

Yes, you might start to feel dizzy after staring for a while. This is because our eyes tend to follow the lines, but then we realize the lines don't lead anywhere. You end up feeling lost. The lines go in all directions, so how do you know which one to follow? You might feel like you're trapped in a whirlwind or a storm.

♦ ♦ ♦

It looks the painter has thrown the paint on the canvas.

Pollock put the canvas on the ground and let the paint pour from holes pierced in tin cans. He turned the pots and directed the colors toward the center, inventing routes for the colors and watching them hit the surface of the painting. Because he used no brushes it looks like the paint itself decided where to fall; but the artist's position and his arm movements actually reduced the element of chance considerably. It was a very controlled process.

How did he get the idea of painting like that?

One of the many European artists who lived as refugees in the United States during the World War II was Max Ernst. Ernst was always experimenting with new techniques. Pollock once visited Ernst's studio and saw him pouring paint onto a canvas to get a spotted effect. Ernst never pursued that technique, but Pollock developed it into the method that became known as dripping.

Did Pollock ever paint in another way?

Yes, he did. He used dripping during a particular period of his work, but his earlier work was very logical. For several years his work included paintings of people and animals fighting. Everything in them was mixed up; then he eventually decided to leave out the people altogether, like they had escaped from his painting or finally reduced each other to dust. All that was left was the chaos.

This painting is strange because you don't know where to look.

Yes, you want to look at everything at once. Your eyes are drawn everywhere at once because no one part of the painting appears to be more important than another. There is nothing more or less at the center of it, and there is no way to tell which is the top and which is the bottom, which is left and which is right. It's unsettling at first, but eventually you have to accept that the usual reference points don't apply here, and that there is no beginning and no end.

Why did he mix everything up like that?

Everything in this picture is mixed up, and it probably makes you feel disoriented. Your eyes are looking for something to latch onto—a recognizable shape or some small element to help you understand what it's all about. That's a normal reaction. Maybe this uncertainty makes you feel annoyed or angry that the painter is being mean to you as a viewer. That kind of emotion is part of what Pollock wanted to convey—just how angry or frustrated we get when we don't understand what is going on.

Do the colors have a particular significance?

The colors don't necessarily have a fixed meaning, but red will usually seem more violent than sky blue; blue will often make you think of the sky; white always seems cleaner than other colors. These are just a collection of feelings implicitly linked to a set of colors. The light blue that serves as a kind of background in this painting could also have been used to cover everything in a different painting.

Why are there so many layers of paint on each other?

The surface of the painting doesn't give us any answers. It's too stormy and featureless for explanations. Perhaps it's better to plunge in, in a sense, and bore down through the layers like an archaeologist excavating earth in search of an image or a fossil. The thickness of the paint suggests an accumulation of geological layers. By penetrating these layers, little by little you find proof that there used to be something else there, even if you can't be sure exactly what it was.

The title doesn't have any relation to what you see.

The numbered part of the title (*Number 3*) places the painting in a sequence of works, done before and after this one. But the fact that it's just a number makes it impossible for a viewer to confirm whether it reproduces something and how. The descriptive part of the title (*Tiger*) is easier to understand: there's savagery, the suppleness of lines, power, a leap, feet, danger. The word *tiger* evokes so many different images and feelings.

Is the painting really supposed to mean something?

At the time when Pollock was working, around World War II, the painting styles then current no longer had any meaning for him. Nothing would have been able to give the feeling of disarray, collapse, with the kind of force he wanted to convey. He couldn't paint actual things breaking down and disappearing because he felt lost in a world where he could no longer recognize anything. But he kept on searching. The painting does not represent ruins: it actually is chaos itself. Everything seems thrown into confusion, lifted here, there, everywhere, without any respite, by the inexhaustible energy of the painting.

₂₇ Untitled Blue Monochrome

Painted 1957; pigment and synthetic resin on canvas mounted on wood
Hamburger Kunsthalle, Hamburg, Germany
Yves Klein
Born Nice 1928; died Paris 1962

Is this really a painting?
Yes, it's a painting, a painting that's all blue.

There isn't anything on it.
Yes, there is—there's blue. The artist chose this color and painted the canvas with it. It's not exactly true to say there's nothing there.

It doesn't look like it's been painted.
You can just make out brushstrokes on the surface like tiny waves. But it's impossible to tell which part was painted first. It almost seems like it turned blue all at once. It didn't, though, of course. It took time to achieve this result. But it seems so simple that it might be hard to believe.

It looks soft.
The surface of the painting isn't shiny; it seems to swallow up light, not reflect it. It looks like, if you touched it, your fingers would sink into it, like velvet. Looking at this painting is relaxing.

It could be the sky.
It is the sky, in a sense. But there is no sun, no clouds, no birds, no wind—none of the normal things that belong in the sky. And it's even bluer than the sky itself. The artist has not described the sky; he has painted the color that suggests it.

Perhaps the artist didn't like other colors.
He had worked with red, yellow, and green before, but, in the end, he chose blue for this painting. According to Klein, blue is the most important color because it evokes the sky and the sea and the idea of infinite space. Rather than being linked to just one thing, it is full of infinite possibilities.

Why did the artist want only one color?
Klein found that, for his work, putting several colors in a painting caused a problem. Even with just two colors, a fight seemed to break out, as if the colors became rivals, each wanting to be the more important, to get more attention, like people talking at the same time. He wanted to create peaceful paintings and found that the solution was to get rid of any risk of conflict. With only one color, that danger was eliminated. This type of painting is called monochrome.

◆ ◆ ◆

Did Yves Klein paint yellow, red, or green monochromes?
Yes, he did. Then he realized that a rivalry was establishing itself between different monochrome paintings. Within each individual picture everything was fine, but a

conflict occurred in the minds of the viewers. For example, someone who had just seen a green painting and then looked at a red one might not be able to forget about the green one. Then, if she saw a yellow one, all three would become mixed up in her head. In the end Klein decided to use to just one color.

Why did he choose blue?
The main reason was that he liked it. There's a lot of blue in Nice, his hometown: it's by the sea and the weather is pleasant. But for him blue, more than any other color, can evoke the intangible, the infinite space of the universe. The colors green or yellow or red can evoke a thousand different shapes and materials—trees, flowers, butterflies, the coolness of grass, the heat of the sun. But to paint with blue is to try to capture emptiness, the very air that holds those flowers and butterflies. You can never grasp it in your hands. It's alluring but elusive, like a dream.

Did he do a lot of other blue paintings?
Yes, he did a huge number of them. They became his universe. In some the paint is lighter or thicker; sometimes it's even in relief. The formats are different from painting to painting. But the color is always identical. Klein found what expressed his artistic vision the best and felt there was no need to change after that.

Does the painting have a frame?
No. If the painting were put in one it would be enclosed, which would contradict the very essence of the idea Klein was trying to convey: it would suggest a prison instead of infinite space and possibility. Without a frame, the painting remains free. Also, when it's displayed in a gallery, the painting isn't hung right up against the wall—it leans forward a little. It seems to float in the air.

People often talk about "I.K.B." when they talk about Klein's paintings. What do these initials stand for?
They are the initials for International Klein Blue, the name given to the color of paint especially made for Klein. Edouard Adam, an ironmonger and artists' supplies merchant in Paris, developed an ideal paint for him: it was a synthetic resin that held its ultramarine blue color without losing any of its brightness over time. The mixture is patented and is not available for commercial use. Sometimes the initials I.K.B. appear in the titles of Klein's paintings, which makes them valuable strictly in regard to the materials in use, regardless of the merits of the painting itself.

What is the point of always painting the same painting?
Rather than thinking of Klein's pictures as repetitions of each other, it is more useful to think of them as pieces of the same image. They follow each other without ever forming a complete whole. Nothing is ever finished or final, and no end is possible. The paintings reflect and answer each other like echoes. The effect is like a poem where the words have been forgotten and all that's left is the rhyme.

Paintings like this don't want to say anything.

Yes, these paintings don't want to say anything or, more accurately, they want to say nothing. It's not that this painting has no meaning: it just refuses to open up or speak. It's not a scene in a play or in a film, and it's not a text either. This painting is an object in its own right, with its own color, shape, and texture. That is what makes it what it is. The artist's will brought it into being, like an element of nature.

It can't be very interesting to see more than one of these.

When you see several blue monochromes together—in an exhibition, for example—you quickly stop thinking of them as identical. They may be identical, but only in the way that windows that are continually opening and shutting are identical. For the first few minutes you try to look for something—who knows what?—then you let go of your ideas, clear your mind, and enter deeper and deeper into the space created by the paintings. You dive into the blue.

What makes this monochrome so special?

On the contrary, monochromatic images, or photographs, are everywhere—in the street, on the television, in newspapers. It's impossible to tell how many we see every day, and each one has its own motivations, movements, shapes and messages. Most other monochromes can't come close to the clarity and purity of a painting like this. An Yves Klein monochrome offers a totally restful place for the eyes and the mind. Looking at one feels like a true luxury.

Did other painters do monochromes?

Klein wasn't the first person to think of painting a monochrome, but his blue paintings brought an aura of serenity to the history of the monochrome. Other artists use the monochrome as a way of saying that there are an infinite number of things still to paint, and they feel full of new beginnings and hope. For other artists, monochromes represent an ending, as though everything has been said and any kind of content has disappeared. There can also be a sense of expectancy, with the monochrome as the calm at the eye of the storm. It all depends on the artist and the period he is working in.

Are paintings with only one color less expensive to buy?

The price of a painting depends on the value set on the artist's work. It doesn't matter if he used one color or several. Taken on its own, a monochrome might not seem very significant. However, the position it takes in the work of the artist and in the history of painting gives it value, reveals its meaning, and justifies its existence.

28 The King of the Zulus

Painted 1984–85; acrylic and mixed media on canvas; 208 x 173 cm
Galeries Contemporaines des Musées de Marseille, France
Jean-Michel Basquiat
Born in New York 1960; died New York 1988

This painting looks like a huge sheet of newspaper.

The artist has combined a number of elements in this painting that might remind us of a newspaper: there's small printed text, faces, and strips of color. He also used splashes of paint that trickle into other images. Like a newspaper, this painting is full of stories.

There's a big mask with its teeth bared.

It's an African mask, but it almost looks more like a real face than a mask. It seems alive, like the face is talking. We don't know why he's showing his teeth. Is it to scare us, because he's laughing, or because he can't help it? Is he scared? Maybe he's angry.

It's a collage.

Collages usually use simple elements from outside the world of art from a variety of sources. This painting juxtaposes elements that don't usually go together, but they were all drawn or painted by the artist himself.

Things are piled on top of one another.

Basquiat lived in New York, a huge city full of people. People jostle each other on the street and in the subways all the time, and sometimes they get hurt. This painting is like that: things squeeze in any way they can; there's not enough room for everything to have its own space. You can see little bits of other pictures weaving their way into the foreground from the background.

The head is very big, but the letters are really small.

The big head might be reading all the little words, but he also might be hearing someone read them or even thinking them. On the other side of the painting, lots of words are piled on top of each other, like a lot of people talking at the same time. All those words combine to form a kind of cacophony, like lots of voices speaking all at once. The other, smaller heads each have lives of their own. They are all doing things, thinking, writing.

It looks like a wall covered in graffiti.
At the beginning of his work as an artist Jean-Michel Basquiat painted on walls in the street. Later he started producing paintings still using the same graffiti style. He wanted his paintings to retain exactly the same characteristics wherever they were, on a wall in a city or in someone's living room. His paintings show reality, the constant mixture that is everyday life: faces, outlines, animals, filth, clashing colors, expressions, curses, doodles, and deletions.

Why is the mask bigger than everything else?
The mask is the heart of the painting, its main character. Originally the artist was going to call the painting *The Brown Mask*, but then the character must have taken on so much importance to him that Basquiat transformed it into a king, the king of the Zulus. He changed the painting's title and the mask became a king. Another way to look at the painting is to understand it as an image of a king surrounded by a crowd of his subjects, and the street is his kingdom. In this sense the king could even be the artist himself.

Why did the artist give the mask an African face?
Jean-Michel Basquiat had a racially mixed background. His father was from Haiti, and his mother was from Puerto Rico. The way he mixes multiple themes in his work addresses his heritage. Instead of being a fusion of different elements, the painting juxtaposes its images, insisting on the plurality of their sources. This is what gives the work an almost random quality, but at the same time gives it great richness. The African face dominates the image and sets the tone; it is emblematic of what the whole painting is about.

Why are the colors so violent?
The important thing about the colors is how they contrast with one another. They are city colors, the colors of cars and billboards, of storefronts and neon signs. Basquiat used acrylic paint that is opaque and shiny like the mass-produced goods we see every day at the store. He used color to create strong associations. Words, regardless of what they actually spell, also play a part in his work. They are written in black and white, giving Basquiat another way to play with the idea of race and color, of the black person in the white man's city.

Why is there so much to read in this painting?

Each piece of writing here has its own tone. If you would read it all, you would become engulfed in a painting of infinite space. Every word, no matter how short or small, suggests images, colors, and sounds. The way the words are arranged together is significant, too. For example, under the mask the word "vent" (the French word for "wind") suggests air blowing around the king; maybe you can feel it with him. Next to the king's ear there is a list of metals: "copper, brass, iron, steel, gold." You can almost hear the noise of the metal, feel how hard it is, whether it is warm or cold, precious or commonplace, or used to make tools, machines, weapons, jewelry. And Basquiat is having fun playing with the words— "copper" can also be slang for "policeman," for example. A whole story is unfolding inside the world of the words. It's up to the viewer to enter it.

This painting looks like it was created really randomly.

Even if the artist has not followed traditional rules of composition, he certainly didn't just throw it together. A dislocated, broken image like this gives off its own kind of rhythm. It kind of feels like rap music, with the same breaks and bursts. Toward the bottom of the painting you can even see a vinyl album, the kind a DJ would scratch as accompaniment to a rapper. Basquiat himself played the clarinet and the keyboard and was also a rapper. With this painting he perfectly captures the sound of the urban streets in the early 1980s.

Graffiti is everywhere, so why should Basquiat's be put in a museum?

Most graffiti, while expressive, is poor quality, limited to repetitive insults or obscenity. Basquiat's work, on the other hand, proves that he has a real talent for composition and for combining very different shapes and references. The links he makes between elements show a deliberate method that's vastly different from the protest or posing you generally see in graffiti. Though he did not study painting or drawing in any formal way, Basquiat was familiar with the art in museums and was friends with other contemporary artists. His works express an extreme violence without being simplistic. When his art began to be accepted by museums, it marked the official recognition of an art form that had turned its back on the fundamental aesthetic tradition in order to develop independently. For Basquiat it was vital to be recognized not only as an artist in his own right but above all as a street artist and a black American painter.

₂₉ Portrait of Isabel Rawsthorne Standing in a Street in Soho

Painted 1967; oil on canvas; 198 x 147.5 cm
Neue Nationalgalerie, Berlin, Germany
Francis Bacon
Born in Dublin 1909; died in Madrid 1992

Where is this strange woman?
The title of the painting tells us she is in a street in Soho, which is an area in central London. It's an ordinary place where she probably goes often; it's just a moment in her everyday life.

You can't see the sidewalk.
She must be crossing the road, which is why you don't see the sidewalk. The artist has shown only the one place that matters to her at that moment, the spot where she is walking.

There's a large yellow circle on the ground.
Maybe it's a large spot of sunlight. It must be a nice day because she isn't wearing a coat. Those large blue shapes at the top of the painting might be the kind of awnings hung out on the street in the summer to protect storefronts and café terraces from the sun.

It looks like the inside of a circus tent.
The round shape on the ground might remind you of a circus ring, and the color might remind you of sand or sawdust. Maybe the artist felt that there isn't much difference between a circus and an ordinary road on an ordinary day: there are all sorts of different people, danger is never far away, and accidents can happen very easily.

What is she doing with her hands?
She is carrying what looks like a purse in her right hand. She's swinging it as she walks, so you can't make it out very clearly—you can only see a few grey lines in the air. It's hard to tell what her other hand is doing. It might be in her pocket or behind her back.

What is she looking at?

She is looking to see if there are any cars coming before she crosses the street. (There is one in the background.) The position of her head also gives us an idea of her state of mind. The artist could have shown her just walking along, but, by choosing the moment when she turns her head, he emphasizes that she's taking an interest in her surroundings and is aware of what is going on around her. She is as alert as the artist observing her.

Why does she have big lines of paint on her face?

The painting doesn't show her face in a same way that a photograph would have. The artist wanted to highlight certain features, so he made up colors and distorted her face. He is not reproducing exactly what he sees, but he's using what he sees as a starting point for the painting. When an artist paints a portrait, he or she applies paint to a canvas. In this painting, her face is truly covered with paint.

What do the straight lines around her represent?

They don't represent one particular thing although they have often been interpreted as the outlines of a box or a transparent cage. This motif often appears in Bacon's work, and he described it as a kind of frame within the painting. It's a way of focusing attention on the figure, of highlighting the person by tightening the space around her.

In the background there is a white shape that looks like an animal's horn.

This shape catches your eye because it is painted with white. In the few places where the artist has used this color, it seems like a violent burst: you can see it by Isabel's left hand, at her feet, on the edge of her dress, on her face, and in the background. That thing that looks like an animal's horn is actually part of a car glinting in the sunlight. But thinking of it as an animal's horn fits with the idea of savagery in the painting. Viewed in this way, the images and their associations start to run into each another: car, wheel, horn, bull, strength, fight, conflict, danger, etc.

Did the artist have someone pose for this painting?

Francis Bacon actually found it embarrassing to paint in front of a model. He realized that, even though he didn't mean it to be, his way of deforming people's faces could be upsetting for them. But, because he was painting a portrait, he still needed to have plenty of contact with his subject. So he made sure he had plenty of photographs to refer to, and tried to see his subject as often as he could. The painting was created from a mixture of physical presence, perception, and memory.

Why is the face painted like a mask?

Bacon was not trying to paint a mask specifically, but he found himself manipulating the face, to show both the actual features of the face and the emotions hidden underneath: he painted both a person and a facade. The layers of color seem like strips of flesh that have been peeled back—the green, white, and pink suggest nerves and tendons. In this sense it's like the mask is being slowly removed. By using this technique, the portrait conveys not only Isabel Rawsthorne's personal pain, but also the general pain of humanity.

Did Frances Bacon do a lot of sketches before painting a portrait?

Bacon didn't do preparatory sketches; whenever he started a painting there was no way of knowing how it would turn out—a bit like life itself. The first few brushstrokes were important because they set the tone for the way the final work would develop. He let the work take its own shape on the canvas, following its own logic, with one shape leading to another. Sometimes he wasn't convinced by the way a painting was developing and there was a tension between what he felt he could control and what he felt was beyond his control. In this painting you can see the results of that tension: the large design with full shapes on the one hand and the little trickle of paint, a little "accident," on the other.

Who was Isabel Rawsthorne?

She was a friend, whom Bacon had met a few years earlier in a bar in Soho (the part of London shown in the painting). She was important to Bacon. In this portrait she is presented as a very strong, compact figure, standing erect, like a pillar. It is significant that Bacon specified her posture in the title, describing her as "standing" in a street. This precision, which he could have omitted, emphasizes how she holds herself upright in this uncertain world. Whatever happens, she acts as a kind of pivot around which other people move as they are passing by.

30 The Girls from Olmo II

Painted October 1981; oil on canvas; 250 x 250 cm
Musée Nationale d'Art Moderne, The Pompidou Centre, Paris, France
Georg Baselitz (known as Georg Kern)
Born at Deutschbaselitz 1938

This painting is upside down.
That's actually how the artist wanted it to look. But yes, it does look like it's upside down.

Could the curator of the museum turn it around?
It's physically possible, but no one really has the right to do that. If the artist has made the decision that it should look like it's upside down, then it should stay upside down. The artist's vision is most important, not anyone else's.

Do I have to stand on my head to look at it?
That might be the first idea that comes to mind, but there's no point. You can just as easily see what the painting is by looking at it this way.

There are two people on bicycles.
Yes, and you can clearly see that they are women. He has made it immediately clear that they are cycling, even though the bicycles are very simply drawn.

The bicycle wheels look like disks.
If you watch a bicycle when it is in motion, it's difficult to make out the spaces between the spokes, so in real life the wheels look like disks, just like they do here.

There's yellow everywhere.
Maybe it's the sun; the painting certainly seems to be full of light and warmth. Maybe that's why they're riding their bikes naked. It is so hot that they don't need clothes.

Their bicycles and their eyes are the same color.
By making them the same color, the artist creates harmony between bicycles and the girls, giving them equal importance. Also, by using the color turquoise, which is a mixture of blue and green, the colors of the sky and nature, he suggests both of these colors in the painting without either of them being visible on its own.

Why do the girls look so like each other?

This isn't a portrait of two specific girls. It's possible that the artist got the idea for the painting by watching several young women riding around on their bicycles. He might have known some of them, but after a while they blended into each other in his mind and he stopped trying to identify them. But the unifying feature was that they were all riding bikes.

Why do they have identical bicycles?

The artist was no more interested in specific bicycles than he was in specific girls; he just wanted to give the idea of bicycles in general. The fact that they are the same color makes the painting feel even simpler. When you are looking at it, you don't notice two different objects. You just understand the idea of "bicycles," and that's enough.

Why are the people and the background the same color?

This painting appears as a block of color. The background and the girls' bodies are the same color and substance, making it difficult to distinguish them. The elements of the painting make a united whole. The figures are so carefully linked to the background it makes it impossible to imagine them in any particular place. You have to accept the world of the painting.

How can the picture be flat but seem to have depth at the same time?

The yellow background doesn't give any indication of place or space. It acts as a kind of opaque wall. But the girls are facing in different directions. The one in the foreground is in profile and she looks like she's getting ready to leave the painting. The other one, on the right, is coming up behind her; we can tell she is farther away because her wheels are smaller. The girl on the right has got her mouth open—maybe she's talking or maybe she's panting. It looks like she's having difficulty keeping up. No matter what the story, they don't just seem stuck onto the painting. It becomes a place where they live and breathe.

Why is it so badly painted?

The picture isn't "badly painted," but the effort that went into creating it is deliberately left visible. The paint has been applied roughly; the brushstrokes are bold and clear. Instead of flattering the subjects, making their shapes smooth, the brushstrokes are a constant reminder of the movements the artist made when he was painting. In places it appears as though it was physically hard work, or even a struggle, for him to bend the paint to his will and produce this picture. All these effects make the subjects look like they've been snatched from reality and that the painting itself has radically altered their appearances. The painting doesn't hide what it's done to them.

What do the words "Olmo II" in the title mean?

Olmo is a small village in Tuscany, Italy. Georg Baselitz used to watch girls cycling there. He painted two paintings on this subject: this one and another painted in October 1981. The colors he chose make it easy to imagine trees in autumn with their leaves turning yellow or red. Olmo was also the last name of a famous Italian cyclist (Giuseppe Olmo), who was a major champion in the 1930s. The name "Olmo" takes on a double meaning for the girls in the painting.

How does Baselitz paint his paintings?

He works with his canvases flat on the ground and approaches the painting from all angles at the same time. In this way he ignores the usual rules of top, bottom, left, right, length, and breadth. He doesn't just paint a painting in one direction and then turn it upside down when it's ready to be to be displayed in a gallery.

Why would someone consider displaying a painting where the image is upside down?

It's actually not unusual for an artist to turn a painting upside down in order to see it better. In this way an artist can look at his or her work objectively and focus on the articulation of color and shape. This is a particularly good test for any painting: when a composition is turned the wrong way, any weaknesses in the composition will become even more obvious. Baselitz has used this technique since at least 1969 to create a new artistic trend.

What is the point in making people look at a painting that's upside down?

Baselitz doesn't force anyone to look at his paintings, whether they are upside down or not. But if you do look at them, you have to be ready to be confronted by something unexpected. Even though the subject is recognizable, its presentation weakens its connection to real life. The link with real life exists, but it is disturbed. Baselitz wants to break down the barriers between figurative art and abstract art. If you look at the painting with an open mind, you might discover that you've completely forgotten that the girls are upside down.

Did Baselitz do this kind of painting to shock people?

It's certainly true that a painting like this won't go unnoticed, but Baselitz didn't set out just to shock people as a goal in itself. Nevertheless, that reaction makes his work even more special. In a world where we are desensitized to photos and films of terrible atrocities, natural disasters, people dying of starvation, and victims of war, torture, and terrorism, this painting manages to shock us simply by showing an image upside down. By provoking a reaction that's disproportionate to its subject, Baselitz is demonstrating the absurdity of our world, which can often feel like it's upside down. This painting reminds us of one of art's most fundamental functions—to take us out of our visual and mental comfort zones.

Photographic credits

ADAGP, Paris, 2002: pages 134, 150, 162, 166, 170

Mondrian/Holtzman Trust c/o Beeldrecht, ADAGP, Paris, 2002: page 154

Succession Chagall, Banque d'Images, ADAGP, Paris, 2002: p.146

Estate of Francis Bacon, ADAGP, Paris, 2002: page 174

AKG, Paris: pages 70, 118, 126

Erich Lessing/AKG, Paris: pages 98, 130, 158

Archives Adam Biro: page 78 (below)

Artephot/J. Martin: page 162

Baselitz George, 2002, Derneburg: page 178

Bildarchiv Preussicher Kulturbesitz/Jörg P. Anders: page 110

Bridgeman Giraudon: pages 62, 78 (above), 94, 106, 142, 166

Bridgeman Giraudon/Lauros: page 174

CNAC/MNAM Dist. RMN: page 178

Kunsthaus, Zurich: page 154

MAC – Galeries Contemporaines des Musées de Marseille: page 170

Photos12.com/ARJ: pages 62, 66, 74, 82, 86, 90, 102, 114, 122, 134, 138, 150

Succession Picasso, Paris, 2002: page 158